PRIVACY AND PROPERTY

THE DAVID HUME INSTITUTE

Hume Papers on Public Policy:
Volume 2 No. 3 Autumn 1994

PRIVACY AND PROPERTY

EDINBURGH UNIVERSITY PRESS

© David Hume Institute 1994

Edinburgh University Press
22 George Square, Edinburgh

Typeset in Times New Roman by ROM-Data Corporation Ltd.,
Falmouth, Cornwall and printed and bound in Great Britain
by Page Bros Limited, Norwich

A CIP record for this book is available from the
British Library

ISBN 0 7486 0593 2

Contents

Contributors

Martin Hogg is a trainee solicitor in Edinburgh.

Dr Alexander McCall Smith is Reader in Law, University of Edinburgh.

Professor W R Cornish is Professor of Law, University of Cambridge.

Professor Antony W Dnes is Professor of Economics, Nottingham Trent University.

Foreword

This collection of papers is broadly united by the themes of privacy and property stated in its title. It brings together the work of four authors currently writing in areas apparently diverse but in fact connected.

In the first paper, Martin Hogg discusses the vexed question of a legal right to privacy, which has been the subject of intense debate in Britain for many years. At the time of writing the publication of a Government White Paper on the subject appeared imminent. Hogg considers the meaning of the term privacy, and the reasons why a problem has developed and why privacy should be respected. The ways in which the law incidentally already recognises and supports privacy are also discussed. He concludes that the law should move to a generalised protection of privacy primarily through the civil (as opposed to the criminal) law, arguing that in Scotland this can be done by development of the existing common law. If statutory reform is deemed necessary, it should be by means of a statement that invasion of personal privacy is an actionable wrong, together with a non-exclusive list of specifically actionable activities. Either technique would be preferable to an extra-legal control such as a press tribunal.

Hogg favours the protection of privacy because individuals wish it so. The next paper, by Alexander McCall Smith, suggests however that there are limits to respect for privacy and individual autonomy. He addresses a question sharply focused by recent cases and legislation: upon what if any grounds is the law justified in taking action to limit an individual's freedom in relation to the use of the body? Three forms of activity may be considered in seeking to answer this question: sado-masochism for sexual gratification, sale of organs for transplantation, and surrogate motherhood. It is argued that the law may legitimately control such activities and limit individual autonomy in respect of them. The basis for this is the principle of dignity, which can be extended to the rejection of degradation and depersonalisation of another even where that other consents to the treatment involved. Some acts are in their essence not private, and interference with individual autonomy to prevent their occurrence is thereby justifiable.

McCall Smith's paper has at its heart the issue of the extent to which the human body may be considered the freely-disposable property of the individual. One of the oldest justifications for intellectual property is that there can be no greater claim to property than over the products of one's own mind. The third contributor, Professor W R Cornish, is one of the world's leading writers on the subject of intellectual property. His paper discusses the position of academic and publicly funded research institutions, which are currently much concerned with intellectual property rights. This is connected with the drive to capitalise commercially upon basic research, and gives rise to issues about the scope of intellectual property, particularly patents. These issues are especially acute in the fields of biotechnology and the patentability of life, notably the human genome. Here again we connect with the themes raised by Hogg and McCall Smith, the justification of claims of "property" and "dignity" in the human body and its attributes. Questions have also arisen about the extent to which such moral issues should be incorporated within patent law and, if allowed, who should be charged with decision-making in these areas. The paper concludes that the development of intellectual property rights in relation to academic research, and the resultant commercialisation of that research, should be supported but must avoid hostility and protest as far as possible. There is a need for education in the nature of intellectual property and its place in the conversion of scientific knowledge to commercial account.

The last paper is by Antony Dnes and serves as an introduction to the economic analysis of law, highlighting in particular the economics of crime with special reference to murder and theft, the property-based wrong of nuisance (which has been one of the bases for the protection of privacy under existing law), and breach of contract. Dnes stresses the contribution which economic analysis of law can make to the study of economics generally, but it could also be said that lawyers in the United Kingdom have so far failed to realise as fully as they might the contribution which economics has made and can make to the analysis and understanding of legal rules and institutions - not least, perhaps, privacy and property.

The David Hume Institute is as ever delighted to be able to publish work which contributes to important current and developing issues of public policy. It is of course necessary to say that the views expressed are the views of the authors alone, and not of the Institute (which as a charity can be committed to no particular line or policy on such questions). But the work of these authors can be safely commended as a worthwhile introduction and contribution to some important debates.

Hector L MacQueen
Executive Director
The David Hume Institute

The Very Private Life of the Right to Privacy

Martin A Hogg

Synopsis

A legally enforceable right to privacy has been the subject of intense debate in Britain. This paper considers the meaning of the term privacy, and the reasons why a problem has developed and why privacy should be respected. The ways in which the law incidentally already recognises and supports privacy are also discussed. The paper concludes that the law should move to a generalised protection of privacy primarily through the civil (as opposed to the criminal) law, arguing that in Scotland this can be done by development of the existing common law. If statutory reform is deemed necessary, it should be by means of a statement that invasion of personal privacy is an actionable wrong, together with a non-exclusive list of specifically actionable activities. Either technique would be preferable to an extra-legal control such as a press tribunal.

* * * *

"I know of no authority to the effect that mere invasion of privacy however hurtful and whatever its purpose and however repugnant to good taste is itself actionable." (Lord Justice-Clerk Thomson, in *Murray v Beaverbrook Papers*, 18th June 1957, unreported)

"...in a democratic society there must be a right to privacy..." (National Heritage Committee 1993: v)

All too often individuals are timid in standing up in defence of their privacy. Yet the incidence of invasions of privacy perpetrated by individuals and organisations against each other has perhaps never been so great as at the present time. Consider the following cases. A young child, while playing naked in the seclusion of a high-walled garden has its photograph taken by a man spying on it; a heavily-drugged individual lying in a hospital room is subjected to questioning and has his photograph taken by a man who has gained entry without permission to the patient's room; two people, one of whom is using a mobile telephone, have their intimate conversation, without their knowledge, taped and then made available to the general public on a premium rate telephone service. Each of the preceding cases surely demonstrates an unacceptable breach of the victim's privacy. Yet none of these infringements of the natural rights of persons was redressable at law in this country, and in none of the cases could the aggrieved party have gone to the courts with a good chance of preventing publication of the offending photographs or recordings. This is unacceptable, and it is now generally felt that the time has come to redress the inadequate protection of personal privacy in the law. As was said in the recent Consultation Paper on *Infringement of Privacy* produced by the Lord Chancellor's Department and the Scottish Office (1993: para 3.13): "the time has now come, as a matter of principle, to recognise in law ... that aspect of personal integrity which we call privacy."

Action on the matter seems, in fact, to be finally imminent. The Consultation Paper has been published, in the wake of the failure of the press to respond to the challenge for better self-regulation made in the first Calcutt Report (1990). Comments on this Consultation Paper were requested by October 1993, and a government White Paper with proposals for legislation is said to be imminent at the time of writing. While these are still forthcoming, it might be helpful to consider where the debate surrounding the protection of personal privacy in the law stands. In particular, I wish to consider: (1) what exactly is meant by the term 'privacy'; (2) the problem that requires addressing; (3) the reasons why privacy should be respected (if any are still in doubt about this); (4) the ways in which the law does already provide incidental protection to privacy; and (5) the possibilities for reform that are available. I propose to consider each of these matters in turn.

The concept of privacy

It seemed for a long time that there would never be any clear understanding or consensus of what was meant by the term 'privacy'. A perpetual problem dogging any discussion of the subject is that there are as many definitions of the notion of privacy as there are commentators on the issue. A further problem has been the difficulty caused in some quarters by treating issues as part of the notion of privacy which do not strictly belong there. For instance, the matter of access to abortion has been considered by some as a privacy matter, when more correctly it concerns questions of liberty. There is another example of this conceptual confusion in the recent US case of *Bowers v Hardwick* 106 S Ct 2841 (1986), which seems to see the right to privacy as an aspect of liberty, and talks both of privacy and liberty. Because of the perceived difficulties in defining the term, some even deserted it altogether, feeling it to be of little value - the position of 'reductionism' (Wacks 1989: 10-11; Younger Report 1972: para 59). In a coherent and well argued paper, however, Ruth Gavison (1980) propounded a tripartite view of the concept of privacy, one which I have previously suggested be seen as an acceptable starting point for analysing the law in Scotland (Hogg 1992). This definition has now been taken up and approved in the Consultation Paper issued by the Lord Chancellor's Department and the Scottish Office (1993: 8-9). Gavison's tripartite definition of privacy, which concentrates on the *concept* of privacy, not the second-order question of a 'right to privacy', sees privacy as encapsulating the notion of the *inaccessibility* of an individual (what is being discussed is *personal* privacy). According to this view, a person enjoys perfect privacy when he or she is completely inaccessible to others. Inaccessibility means (1) no-one has any information about the individual, (2) no-one pays any attention to him or her, and (3) no-one has physical access to him or her. Personal privacy thus relates not only to our seclusion from physical interference or attention from others, but also to extensions of ourselves which have significance socially and legally, namely information about us.

Interference with or attention paid to our personal property may also raise questions of privacy. The boundaries of this further aspect may at first appear a little more difficult to define, however. Does someone diminish your privacy by rifling through your possessions even if he gains no information about you? I think, arguably, he does. If someone gains access to your home whilst you are absent, does his very presence breach your privacy? Again I consider it does so. But I think that there must be an element of breaching the boundaries of a place set aside as private; there would be no breach of privacy if an individual handled or looked at private property which was on public view or not set aside in a private place. The mere fact that the property is personal is not therefore enough: the breacher of privacy must invade some *cordon privé* which has been erected around the property. I think it is important to bear this further aspect of privacy in mind, and it is an extension which I would suggest to Ruth Gavison's concept of privacy.

Having formulated a definition of the concept of privacy, it is then possible to talk in terms of a *right to privacy*: that is, the right of an individual to the state of inaccessibility which has been mentioned, or, one might say, the right to demand of others that this privacy not be diminished by them. This is, of course, a second-stage question and involves value judgments and moral arguments. Should one be entitled to privacy in a given situation? Should not the competing claim or right of another prevail over the claimed right to privacy? These are questions of balancing privacy against other interests, and are considered below as part of the problem surrounding privacy. What should be recognised to begin with is that privacy is a concept capable of adequate definition and discussion. In a legal system which valued privacy for its own sake, one would expect to find treatment of such a concept. To date, this has been sadly lacking both in Scotland and England.

The concept of privacy discussed above has, however, been attacked on the basis that it suggests that any diminution of any of the components of privacy would require to be seen as an invasion of privacy (Wacks 1989). This is quite correct, but the criticism has no real sting to it, because what is crucial is not to recognise mere invasions of privacy, but those which should then be actionable at law. Recognising the mere invasion is a first step; deciding on whether it should be actionable raises questions of the level of privacy which one is entitled to expect in a given situation, and the balancing of other competing rights and interests. Clearly a subjective evaluation by individuals of when their privacy invasions should be actionable would not be acceptable.

I would suggest that the level be set by reference to the reasonable expectations of an individual in a given situation, and the nature of the diminution of privacy. By this latter factor, which impacts on the first, I mean, for instance, the character of the information discovered (in other words, it must be of a private, personal nature), or the locus of the invasion (such as one's own home, or even an area set apart as private in the midst of a public space, such as a changing room, locker, or hospital room), or the repeated nature of an action (such as repeatedly telephoning or pestering an individual). Revealing to others what an individual has been doing in a non-private setting may thus conceptually diminish privacy by reducing that individual's inaccessibility to others in informational terms, but it should not be worthy of redress at law as the event reported will have occurred in a non-private setting.

The problem of the lack of protection of privacy

The problem which has presented itself in the United Kingdom in a very clear and undisputable manner is that individuals, both in the public eye and less publicly, have increasingly been subjected to invasions of their privacy without sufficient means of redress. While it has always been accepted that freedom of speech is an important right in a free society, it has become evident that respect for the right to privacy, for so long accepted as part of the mores of society, has been breaking down. Individuals and organisations have been freely breaching others' privacy with impunity, for gain or for mere spurious interest. And when the law has been pushed on the subject, it has given little solace to individuals as far as their claims for an *explicit* right to privacy have been concerned.

It is true that privacy, as a concept and value, is an element of greater or lesser importance in various proceedings of the Scottish (and English) courts. For instance, in relation to the admission of press reporters to certain judicial proceedings, it has been said that

> under section 20 of the Criminal Procedure (Scotland) Act 1975, the guiding principle will be that of privacy, from which it follows that the press will be excluded unless Parliament has said otherwise (*Sloan v B* 1991 SLT 530 at 551).

And in the Scottish Land Tribunal, the concept of privacy is on occasions relevant to the proceedings, as it was in *McMillan v Strathclyde Regional Council* 1984 SLT (Lands Trib) 25, where a witness for the claimant (who was attempting to show that a proposed course of action would inflict material detriment on his property) gave evidence that, in his opinion, the privacy of the house in question would be affected by passers-by. Other cases could be cited in which privacy is relevant, many of these bringing in a public law dimension. For instance, *Leach v Secretary of State for Scotland* 1991 SLT 910 concerned the right to the privacy of communication between a prisoner and his solicitor, and also highlights the fact that one's status may be relevant to the degree of privacy to which one is entitled. Such cases indicate that privacy may be a relevant factor for a court in reaching a decision, and that privacy can sometimes be viewed as a component right in a larger, compound concept, such as the group of rights which go to make up the notion of property (see further below, 17-21). However, where the law has been asked to make a decision on an action for breach of privacy alone, it has not given a favourable response, as I have already noted.

One can think of many recent examples of invasions of privacy which have proved irremediable in the British courts. I alluded at the beginning of this paper to the photographing of the infant Princess Eugenie and the actor Gordon Kaye, as well as to the tape recording of a conversation alleged to have occurred between the Princess of Wales and a friend. Other cases will be remembered: the photographs of a topless Duchess of York and a friend; the telephone conversation between the former Minister David Mellor and the actress Antonia de Sancha; and the revelations about the politicians Virginia Bottomley and Paddy Ashdown. Recently there has been the publicity surrounding the 59-year old woman who gave birth to twins after artificial impregnation (*The Scotsman*, 1 January 1994), and the allusions in a television advertisement to Mr Norman Lamont's alleged purchases in an off-licence. There has also been, most recently, the possibility of the publication of photographs of a topless Princess of Wales and of Prince Edward and his girlfriend, the latter of which prompted a complaint by Buckingham Palace to the Press Complaints Commission. There are less well-known examples of invasions of privacy, such as that of the woman forced to remove her brassière in a police cell, which formed the subject matter of the case of *Henderson v Chief Constable of Fife* 1988 SLT 361. No doubt many other examples could be cited. I do not suggest that all such invasions of privacy be considered actionable, but let it at least be acknowledged that privacy has been invaded.

Cases such as these prompted another attempt to introduce privacy legislation. On 11th May 1994, Lord Harman Nicholl attempted to introduce the Photographs and Films (Unauthorised Use) Bill into the House of Lords, but this was defeated. Furthermore, in July 1994 the British Medical Association published a survey of nearly 100 health authorities and NHS trusts which revealed a long list of disclosures of personal information by medical authorities. As a consequence, the BMA also published a code for respecting medical privacy in the form of draft legislation, in an attempt to promote rectification of such breaches of medical privacy by health authorities.

Analysed in the abstract, there are a number of ways in which a breach of privacy may be committed for which no real or sufficient redress exists in the current law. Amongst others could be cited:

(1) spying on and/or photographing an individual without his or her knowledge or consent whilst that individual is on private property;

(2) audio/visual recording of an individual whilst he or she is in private property and without his or her knowledge or consent;

(3) in the absence of a relationship of confidence, copying private letters or documents without consent (save as protected under copyright - see further below, 17-18), and disseminating the information contained in such;

(4) the *recording* of telephone calls made by means of a public telecommunications system, a term now including cellular operators' systems (though *monitoring* such calls, which would be a pre-requisite, is an offence under the Interception of Communications Act 1985);

(5) non-consensually gaining access to another on private property, the law of trespass being wholly ineffective to combat this.

That the law will not provide an adequate remedy in many cases may be seen from statements in several cases. In *Kaye v Robertson* [1991] FSR 62 the court held that there was no action for invasion of privacy in English law. A similar remark was made by Lord Justice-Clerk Thomson in the unreported case of *Murray v Beaverbrook Papers*, quoted at the head of this paper. However, in some of the above cases, remedies were available to the aggrieved parties. The Duchess of York obtained damages for the photographs taken of her in France, where laws on privacy do exist; Norman Lamont had the offending advertisement removed from the television, the Independent Television Commission ruling that it had invaded his privacy; and the name of the 59-year old woman who gave birth to the twins was banned from publication in the press, Mr Justice Ewbank of the English High Court saying that the balance that had to be met between freedom of the press and the family's right to privacy "falls heavily in favour of privacy" (*The Scotsman*, 1 January 1994). What these cases show is that it is possible to provide a sensible protection of privacy: there is no reason therefore why all such cases should not be capable of being judged in the British courts, should the requisite level of invasion of privacy or impending invasion be reached. It should not be necessary to have to rely on the jurisdiction of foreign courts, or the non-legally binding decisions of independent commissions.

The principal objection to protection of privacy: competing rights would suffer

The protection of privacy in the United States of America, especially at a constitutional level, provides a good example of a problem which arises wherever privacy is protected, that of balancing privacy against other rights. In the USA, the right to privacy has continually vied with the right to freedom of speech. Privacy has been developed from guarantees in the Constitution (see *Griswold v Connecticut* 381 US 510, 1965) as well as in the law of tort and by statute; freedom of speech is guaranteed in the First Amendment to the Constitution. The US courts now tend to favour an approach of tackling each case on its facts and are reticent to lay down sweeping principles to apply in all cases where rights have to be balanced (see *The Florida Star v BJF* 105 L Ed 2d 443, 1989). This approach of balancing rights may also be seen from the conflict of values expressed in Articles 8 and 10 of the European Convention of Human Rights and, in the United Kingdom, in those areas of the law which can be used to protect privacy (such as breach of confidence): concerns such as the interest of the public in preventing evasions of the law (*R v IRC ex parte*

Rossminster Ltd [1980] 2 WLR 15), in discovering the truth so that justice may be done (*Riddick v Thames Board Mills* [1977] QB 881), and the right of the press to inform the public (*Schering Chemicals Ltd v Falkman Ltd* [1981] 2 WLR 848), have operated so as to diminish personal privacy.

I have already mentioned the comment of Mr Justice Ewbank in the case of the 59-year old artificially-impregnated woman, which indicates that judges who are given the opportunity to consider matters of privacy are well aware of the need to consider other important rights such as freedom of speech and of expression. The legitimate claims of persons to a right to free speech or expression must be raised and considered wherever they apply in cases of invasion of privacy, but they should not be allowed to defeat at the starting post equally valid claims to a right to privacy. A certain amount of balancing and compromise will be inevitable, with one right perhaps prevailing in any given case. But this is a common feature of the law and one the courts are well used to dealing with. The argument which has been put forward by some (e.g. Bonnington 1992), that our courts could not cope with such a balancing exercise, simply does not fit with the facts, as the courts are faced every day with balancing people's interests, not least of all in such areas of law as family law, breach of confidence, and trade restrictions. The issue of how one weighs the balance in a particular case must, I think, be left for the most part to be decided by consideration of the facts of the case. Of course, a law of privacy developed at common law or in statute may provide guidelines. For instance, one consideration might be that an individual is a public figure, and as such a public figure must be prepared to accept a higher degree of publicity than private individuals. Caveats should be clearly defined, however, as this one was by Sir David Calcutt who observed in his *Report on Press Self-Regulation* (1993: para 4.38) that while

> everyone is entitled to protection of their privacy, those persons discharging public functions must be prepared to expect the level of that protection to be reduced to the extent, but only to the extent, that it is necessary for the public to be informed about matters directly affecting the discharge of their public functions.

I would agree with this statement, and note that the requirement that the matter relate *directly* to the public functions of the individual would raise doubts as to the legitimacy of publishing many of the stories contained in the press about the private lives of public figures. The justification often used to back up the publication of these, that the matter relates to their public office by relating to their trustworthiness in some way, seems to me only doubtfully tenable.

There are other considerations which could be adduced to sway the matter more in favour of privacy or publicity, but, for the moment, I would restate firstly that there is a problem relating to privacy, which is that it is not adequately protected as a separate right in the law; and secondly that the frequently cited objection that one cannot protect privacy without destroying a right to free speech or expression is very dubious.

The reasons why privacy should be respected

Privacy should be protected above all because individuals wish it to be so. Elizabeth von Arnim has a character in one of her novels reflecting that

> What she wanted, what she surely had a right to, was privacy. She had no wish to intrude on the others; why then should they intrude on her? (von Arnim 1992: 131-2)

This is a natural sentiment and one felt by all individuals at various points in their lives. It is of course true that privacy taken to excess may be damaging to the social life of an individual, and may on occasions be used as a cloak to cover up misdeeds, but it is surely undisputed that all human beings require a degree of privacy for their well-being and are entitled to require this from others. Even in societies in which the family group is extended more widely than in our own and may be gathered together in one location, a certain amount of privacy is still seen as necessary. Indeed privacy must be seen as a *human right*, with all the implications which that term carries.

I would include amongst the goods which privacy promotes, the following: relaxation; self-reflection and consideration; the opportunity for the attainment of greater knowledge; self-expression (enabling the lowering of the individual's public face); development of personal relationships with another (in which case the first person necessarily consents to reduce his privacy to the extent of being with the second, but no further), including through conversation, enjoyment of physical proximity, touch, and sexual behaviour; the promotion of a sense of personal well-being; meditation, contemplation and prayer; the relief of stress, through the ability to engage in conduct not permitted in public, the breaking of social taboos, or the release of emotion; mental stability, in that a well-balanced personality requires a certain amount of time to itself; and simple enjoyment, of the state of solitude or of the foregoing goods.

While many of the above goods may be achieved in a 'public' setting, some may not and many are not achieved with such ease as in private. To deny an individual a right to privacy, that is, a claim to have this privacy enforced against intrusion by others, is thus to damage that individual and to fail to respect him or her as a human being. While the law may require privacy to be reduced or taken away in certain cases for the good of society as a whole, or in order to uphold basic rights of other human beings, to fail to provide any explicit legal protection for privacy as a coherent concept, worthy of protection for its own sake, is a failing which any legal system should be required to address. As we have seen above, the Scottish and English legal systems stand accused of this charge. It is to tackling this problem that I wish to turn in the final section of this paper, but before doing so I wish to consider ways in which the law, albeit often haphazardly and by accident, can be presently used to afford protection to privacy. While the law has refused to protect privacy for its own sake, where privacy exists in conjunction with other rights or interests, ways have been found to afford it protection.

Current incidental protection of personal privacy

While the law still ponders the provision of explicit protection for privacy, it is instructive to examine aspects of Scots law which can currently play a role in privacy protection and may still serve some purpose even after the introduction or development of a specific right. I wish to say something about the civil law of contract, delict, and property, as well as the criminal law, in order to consider specific aspects which may provide protection for privacy; I will also touch briefly on the importance of statutory protection. Not every incidental protection offered by the law will protect all three of the aspects of privacy mentioned above, and this should be borne in mind as a remedy or action is discussed.

I: Contract

The law of contract could conceivably be used to cover all aspects of privacy. It is most likely, however, to be used to protect the privacy of personal information. A contract designed explicitly to impose an obligation to respect personal privacy is quite possible (subject to public policy considerations, and the rule against trivial undertakings). An example of such an agreement arose in *Dalgleish v Lothian & Borders Police Board* 1992 SLT 721, decided in the Outer House of the Court of Session. Quite apart from the delictual ground of breach of confidence which Lord Cameron of Lochbroom was prepared to accept as existing (1992 SLT at 724H), employees of a police authority were able to point to an agreement undertaken by the authority (1992 SLT at 722J) not to disclose certain information held about them. This was an example of an agreement not to breach the private nature of personal information, and indicates how the law of contract may be used to protect privacy. Such agreements occur frequently in the realm of employment, not merely in order to bind employers, but employees also (although in the latter case the subject matter is mostly trade secrets, something which is tangential to personal privacy and which I do not propose to discuss here).

A specific term in a contract the general subject of which is not primarily concerned with privacy may deal with the protection of privacy. This is often the case in financial agreements, banker-customer facilities, and credit agreements. Such terms are often expressed as aspects of confidentiality: in the realm of information especially, the terms confidentiality and privacy seem to take on very similar aspects.[1] This, therefore, is an aspect of the law of confidence, and one which may protect privacy.

Additionally, one may find in the case law relationships (here I restrict myself to ones which stem from a contract) in which the obligation of confidence may be implied. Particular relationships in which this presumption of confidentiality has arisen in the case law include that between a photographer and his customer (*McCosh v Crow* (1903) 5 F 670), an accountant and his client (*Brown's Trustees v Hay* (1898) 25 R 1112), a doctor and his patient (*AB v CD* (1851) 14 D 177), and between spouses (*Argyll v Argyll* [1967] 1 Ch 303). Given that the first of these relationships is one which is short-lived, a commercial transaction for the provision of services, it may be possible to conclude that any contractual relationship (and not merely 'professional' ones) in which sensitive personal information or material is being dealt with may give rise to this presumption of confidentiality. It is interesting to note that in the early case of *McCosh v Crow* (1903) 5 F 670 the obligation of confidence implied between photographer and customer was held to bind a successive proprietor of the photographer's business still in possession of the photographs in question. This is an unusual example of a contractual obligation of confidence binding a third party long before the reasonable man principle was developed in the delictual law of confidence (see further below, 12-15). Another noteworthy feature of the case is Lord Moncrieff's comment that the right to veto the exhibition of the picture did not depend upon any prejudice or damage to the pursuer ((1903) 5 F at 680), a fact which enhances the protection of privacy which the case supports.

Certain factors limit the usefulness of the law of contract for the protection of privacy. These are principally (i) that it provides no redress against third parties who might breach privacy (the case of *McCosh* may be incorrect so to suggest, though Lord Ross certainly referred to it in uncritical terms in *Lord Advocate v Scotsman Publications* 1988 SLT 490); and (ii) there is the practical difficulty of contracting with all the possible parties who may breach privacy in respect of the matter in question, and of providing for all possible privacy-diminishing scenarios.

II: General principles of delict

Before looking at individual, nominate delicts, it is instructive to enquire whether under the general principles of delict, an invasion of privacy might be actionable.

It has been said of the delictual law of South Africa, a 'mixed' legal system like that of Scotland, that its essential characteristic is that it is founded upon general principles of liability, in contrast to the casuistic approach of English law, and that

> In general... the South African law of delict is founded on the basic principle that all harm caused by wrongful and blameworthy (or culpable) conduct can be recovered by delictual action (Joubert 1976- : **8**, *Delict*, para 2).

This approach is comparable to that of Scots law. In the authoritative Erskine's *Institutes* (1871: III,i,13), under the title on obligations arising from delinquency, we find it stated that

> every fraudulent contrivance or unwarrantable act by which another suffers damage, or runs the hazard of it, subjects the delinquent to reparation

and Stair, in his *Institutions* (1981: I,ix,6), talks of general obligations of delinquence, which are "pursued under the general name of damage and interest" and have "as many branches and specialities, as there can be valuable and reparable damages". Of course, for any conduct to lead to liability it must first be classifiable as a harm or a wrong, and while it may be true that the "[k]inds of conduct which may cause harm... are infinite" (Walker 1981: 5), for any conduct to be classed as wrongful, it seems that it must affect a recognised remediable interest of the individual. It has not to date been certain in the eyes of the courts whether the interest in privacy is such an interest, any conduct breaching which may be classified as wrongful. The interest in physical integrity is such an interest, and may on occasions be used to protect privacy. A good example of this is *Khorasandjian v Bush* [1993] QB 727, in which one line of reasoning provided protection for the plaintiff's privacy by restating that liability exists in England for causing physical harm (including mental shock) by verbal threats uttered with such an intention, and by extending that principle to cover a case where mental shock was considered likely and stress was already manifested. Clearly this is of use for privacy protection, but it is not protecting privacy *simpliciter*, but physical integrity. Calcutt (1990: para 12.2) was clearly of the opinion that it would be a permissible development to view privacy as a remediable interest:

> A common law right to privacy could possibly develop in Scotland, where there is a more general concept of culpa... compared with the more narrowly-drawn English torts.

That the law has to date set itself against remedying mere invasions of privacy is true with one recent exception taken into account. In one case in the Outer House of the Court of Session, the court seems, albeit on an *ad hoc* basis, to have taken tentative steps in remedying an invasion of privacy based upon such general principles. The case in question is *Henderson v Chief Constable of Fife* 1988 SLT 361. Though this is only an Outer House case, it seems to be a clear example of an award of damages for a mere invasion of privacy. In this case, a woman in police custody was asked to remove her brassière by a police officer, an act described by Lord Jauncey as "an invasion of privacy" and as "not justified in law". The woman was awarded £300 as compensatory damages on the basis that the act was an invasion of privacy and liberty. The case does, however, provide little analysis as to the reasoning behind the decision, and a reader of the decision is left guessing as to the principles underlying it. There are several other cases, cited by the Scottish Law Commission in its *Memorandum on Confidential Information* (1977: para 56) as instances of the *actio iniuriarum*, which may in fact be instances of liability for breach of privacy under general delictual principles. The Scottish courts have as yet to view these isolated cases in any coherent way, though it would be a welcome and logical step for them to do so.

Such a generally recognised delictual principle of breach of privacy would need to be developed through further case law in order to determine its breadth and the exceptions to the obligation. Such development could draw on the experience of the law of delict in relation to causation, damages, and so forth. In any such development, Scots law would be working from a legitimate base, the general principles of delict and the small number of cases suggesting a delictual action for invasion of privacy providing the foundation.

Development of the common law is a route which has been pursued in other jurisdictions. A recent statement of the applicability of the law of delict to the problem of the protection of privacy was made in New Zealand, in the case of *Bradley v Wingnut Films* [1993] 1 NZLR 415. While the plaintiff lost his action for an injunction to prevent dissemination of the defendant's film which included shots of a gravestone owned by the plaintiff, the High Court of New Zealand made a clear commitment to protecting privacy in principle. Mr Justice Gallen was prepared to accept that a cause of action in tort for breach of privacy existed in New Zealand, though he did add that its development should proceed with caution. This statement of principle came after a period of long uncertainty in New Zealand as to the status of the right to privacy, but indicates that development of the common law may provide a route to protect the right, with development proceeding on a case by case basis. Mr Justice Gallen recognised the need to balance the right against other rights, principally the right to freedom of expression.

Such a development may, though, be less likely in Scotland now that the government is considering legislating in this area. In any case, if the common law were to undergo any development such as that outlined, this would be by a process over a period of time. Which nominate delicts, therefore, may play a useful role in the protection of privacy? It should be said at this point that I consider that any statutory action in the protection of privacy should take the form of a general delict of invasion of privacy, rather than extending existing delicts or creating new narrow ones, an approach which merely addresses the topic piecemeal. The approach of the courts in cases such as *Khorasandjian v Bush* in the meantime displays ingenuity in protecting against such privacy diminishing acts as verbal harassment by extending existing nominate delicts to cover new situations.

III: Nominate delicts: breach of confidence

The suitability of the delict of breach of confidence as a means of protecting individual privacy has been criticised (Wacks 1989: ch 3 and passim). Some of the detailed points made in such criticisms are considered below, but two general criticisms may be considered first. It has been said that (i) breach of confidence is "conceptually grounded in policy considerations which, for the most part, require a strained interpretation in cases involving non-technical information" (Wacks 1989: 131-2); and (ii) that the action is concerned with disclosure and/or use rather than publicity, and with the preservation of confidences rather than with harm caused to the plaintiff (Wacks 1989: 134). The first point does not seem to be borne out by the not insubstantial number of cases dealing with information of a non-technical nature, to which the action has been easily suited, and by the long history of cases involving confidences in recognised relationships (MacQueen 1993: paras 1458, 1466). In response to the second point, neither criticism is really a denial of the suitability of the action to protecting privacy: in fact, if the action is available at the point of disclosure, and can be raised without the need to show detriment, then this is beneficial for privacy protection.

The action for breach of confidence is, of course, restricted to breaches of privacy taking the form of the disclosure of confidential information, and thus affects principally only one of the three aspects of privacy outlined earlier. Several factors make it useful in such protection, however, and I wish, accordingly, to look at this nominate delict in some detail:

(a) Breach of confidence: the breadth of the general principle

A formulation for the reasonable person test applicable in Scots law that has recently been proposed would import the obligation of confidence where the recipient should as a reasonable person have realised in all the circumstances that he was bound to treat the information as confidential (Scottish Law Commission 1984; MacQueen 1993: para 1459). Now, if one accepts that certain information may, by its very nature, be considered private and confidential (such as that about one's intimate personal life), then if such information were to come into another's hands, it is arguable that a reasonable person could only assume that she or he was bound to respect its confidential nature. The information would, of course, require to have the necessary quality of confidentiality, something which might arise arguably either because the two parties agree it to have such quality or, even in the absence of any agreement between parties, because it is of a certain nature. The 'nature' of the information would appear to require that it be at least inaccessible to the public (Gurry 1984: 70). Something more seems to be necessary, however, for as MacQueen (1993: para 1460) notes, the fact that the public is generally ignorant about something does not make it confidential. Some other factor must be required, though it is hard to see exactly what it is. It may be that it is the attitude of the confider[2] and/or the class of information to which the material belongs - e.g. details about one's sex life.[3]

It will be hard for the reasonable person to realise in all circumstances if information is confidential. Such a person has, in a sense, to pre-guess the court's findings in any possible action concerning it. It would be best for him or her to err on the side of caution, thus providing greater protection for privacy. The potential use for privacy protection of a wide reasonable person principle will be evident.

(b) Breach of confidence: the types of information covered

Despite criticisms made by some (Wacks 1989: 100), it seems that this factor is really irrelevant. Any kind of information is capable of being confidential, though, of course, certain kinds may more easily raise a presumption of confidentiality under the reasonable person principle.

(c) Breach of confidence: continuance of the obligation over time

As has been said, "there is no time limit on the duration of the right [of confidence]" (MacQueen 1993: para 1452), a fact which enhances the protection it offers to privacy. Unlike other obligations, it does not prescribe.

(d) Breach of confidence: no requirement of detriment?

The absence of the need for the pursuer to show detriment would be of benefit to privacy protection. Often no harm will have occurred, as an interdict may be sought to prevent such happening. In such cases, it would be nonsensical to suggest that harm was a necessary prerequisite of action (though the question of the apprehension of harm is a different matter). The authorities on the requirement of detriment apart from this are mixed, some for, some against. In the Spycatcher case there are persuasive *obiter* comments that it is not. Even if it were a requirement, one would want to ask if hurt to feelings were classifiable as such detriment. There is no clear authority on this, though given that disclosure of private information might conceivably cause emotional distress alone, there is a good case for saying that this should be seen as sufficient detriment.

Having looked at factors which may enhance the scope of breach of confidence actions for privacy protection, it must be recognised that several factors similarly restrict it:

(i)   As has been noted, it is primarily useful only with regard to the *informational* aspect of privacy protection. Of course, a confidence may be breached in circumstances which also involve the aspects of physical access or attention, but in the absence of information disclosed the action would be irrelevant.

(ii) A *relationship of confidence* is a prerequisite of the action. As has been suggested, however, the reasonable person test may catch a wide class of persons, thus lowering the hurdle of this requirement. The courts have not yet fully taken on board the full implications of this test for the class of defenders who may be caught. It would be interesting to see if, accepting that photographs may constitute information, an action could be sustained against a person taking an intrusive, secretive photograph of another, say, in a compromising position.

(iii) There must be a *use or disclosure (actual or threatened) of the information*. This puts the level of actionability at that of 'use' at least. But privacy is breached at the moment of the obtaining of the information, something which would appear to be irremediable under the present law of confidence.

(iv) Only the person to whom the obligation is owed may bring an action for breach of that obligation. Thus, in *Fraser v Evans* [1969] 1 QB 349 the plaintiff was held unable to sue as no duty was owed to him. There is a danger then that if personal information concerns someone but they themselves are not owed the obligation of confidence that they may be left without a remedy when their personal details are spread abroad. However, a case such as *Stephens v Avery* [1988] 2 All ER 477 indicates that if the nature of the information and other circumstances suggest that a reasonable person ought to be aware of its confidentiality, then a remedy may be available to the person about whom the information relates. Adoption of the reasonable person principle broadens the class of persons having title to sue.

(v)   Innocent use or disclosure is generally held not to incur liability (MacQueen 1993: para 1476), though if one has subconsciously used or disclosed information which is the subject of an obligation of confidence then liability will arise (MacQueen 1993: para 1476). Those cases in which the privacy of confidential information will be innocently breached are likely to be fairly infrequent, however.

(vi) Perhaps the biggest potential restriction on the usefulness of the action for breach of confidence in protecting privacy is the defence of public interest. This has been cited by some as a potential disaster for a privacy law, as this factor would no doubt operate as a defence in privacy cases as it does in breach of confidence, and it is feared that this might negate any benefits for privacy otherwise gained. I doubt this to be the case however. I have already said elsewhere that an examination of recent breach of confidence cases indicates that in more cases than not the defence of public interest has actually failed. This is despite its success in some headline cases. It would, moreover, be misleading to suggest that only a defender may cite the concept of the public interest. In the recent case of *Parks v Tayside Regional Council* 1989 SLT 345, in a discussion on the production of confidential information, it was judicially remarked that

> The interest of an individual in his own privacy is itself a public interest. Any breach of confidentiality which infringes the individual's right to his own privacy is accordingly to some extent at least a breach of public interest.

Not only does this provide ammunition for a pursuer in utilising the notion of the public interest, but it specifically mentions the interest of privacy as part of the notion of the public interest, and thus adds weight to the case for recognising privacy as an autonomous legal consideration.

Even if the above comments on the public interest are doubted, the notion could be adapted in any privacy law to a more restrictive sense if this was thought necessary. It could be stated exactly which component matters were to make up the public interest. Thus, relevant factors might be that the pursuer was a public figure and the revelations related to his public duty, or that, as a public figure, the pursuer was portraying himself in a false light, or, more broadly, that the matter was one affecting the public health, the economy, or the security of the nation. In any case, I am not convinced that the public interest defence is a fatal one for either the use of breach of confidence in protecting privacy, or in any possible right of action for breach of privacy alone.

IV: Nominate delicts: Verbal injury: the actio iniuriarum

This area of the law, for so long neglected, was in recent years the subject of a helpful reconsideration by Kenneth Norrie (1985). I do not intend to dwell on the area at great length, for the *actio iniuriarum* suffers now from a restricted application. The action, developed in Scots law from the Roman law at the time of the institutional writers, was at first available for a wrong committed in contempt of an individual's fame or reputation (and according to some writers, in contempt of dignity also). The action as it developed came to focus on damage caused by verbal injury, rather than the earlier alternative of real injury. The neglect of this latter aspect of real injury poses a problem for the protection of privacy, as it excludes such actions as assault, unauthorised taking or publication of photographs, breaking into a person's home, spying on another and so forth, which could have been available under a wider notion of the *actio iniuriarum*. The potential of the *actio iniuriarum* is seen in its use in South African law. There, the *actio iniuriarum* has been developed to permit privacy invasions involving insult to an individual's person, dignity or reputation to be remedied, and would extend to all three aspects of the tripartite notion of privacy developed by Gavison. There have been cases on, amongst others, spying on individuals (*R v Holliday* 1927 CPD 395), disrupting a private meeting between a lawyer and his client (*Ramsay v Minister van Polisie* 1981 (4) AA 802), and publishing photographs of another without permission (*O'Keefe v Argus* 1954 (3) CPD 244 and *Mhlongo v Bailey* 1958 (1) WLD 370). This approach could be adopted in Scots law, but is less likely than the avenue under general delictual law, as a certain widening of the scope of the *actio iniuriarum* in current Scots law would have to be pursued. The Scottish Law Commission (1977) have suggested that the *actio iniuriarum* could still be used to remedy real injuries, but I doubt whether the Scottish courts would seriously consider pursuing this road.

V: Nominate delicts: Defamation

The conclusion of the Lord Chancellor's Department and the Scottish Office (1993) on this action as a means of protecting privacy was that it "does not adequately safeguard a person's privacy" (para 4.11), a comment with which I would agree. The principal drawback of the action is the defence of *veritas* (that the statement complained of was true), and this could easily be raised at the stage of interdict to thwart an attempt to prevent the statement complained of from being published. Indeed, one could argue that privacy is not really infringed *per se* by the false statements which might be made about someone, even if the attendant publicity would amount to a breach of privacy. The action for defamation is only of relevance to the informational aspect of privacy, another restricting factor. If a delict of privacy invasion were developed, it is likely that defamation would be considered an inappropriate action where the thrust of the complaint was in fact invasion of privacy. Indeed, Mr Justice Gallen in *Bradley v Wingnut Films*, mentions, in respect of certain of the plaintiff's pleadings, that "it becomes clear that the situation is much more analagous with an action for defamation than one for breach of privacy" ([1993] 1 NZLR at 424). While a breach of privacy may contain false revelations and defamation could thus be a useful tag on which to hang an action, the requirement of falsity is a restrictive one for a pursuer seeking redress for a privacy invasion.

VI: Property law

In turning to the law of property, I leave behind for the moment the realm of obligations and rights *in personam*, and consider the different legal territory of rights *in rem*. For property to be of use in the protection of privacy, some item of property must be part of the factual background to the diminution of privacy. While this poses, as will be shortly seen, some problems for the attention and physical access aspects of privacy, the problems are even greater for the informational aspect of the interest. It is this latter aspect to which I turn first of all.

(i) Information as property

There has been some discussion of whether confidential information may be considered either intellectual property, or property in general terms (MacQueen 1993: paras 1452-3). The notions of *confidential* information and *private* information are not synonymous, but to the extent that they are both types of information which may be recognised by reference to certain similar qualities attached to them ("confidential" and "private"), it is submitted that the discussions as to whether they may be property are largely applicable one to the other.

MacQueen (1993: para 1453), in his discussion on confidential information, concludes that "it seems best in the current state of the law not to regard confidential information as having all the consequences of property." This seems true of private information also: it is not property such that one can be prevented from using or possessing it. There is Scottish and English authority, however, which suggests that where unpublished, private information has been disclosed to only a small group of persons, the originator of the information may still be able to retain certain rights over it (inter alia, *Cadell & Davies v Stewart* (1804) Mor, App. 'Literary Property', No 4; *Prince Albert v Strange* 2 De G & SM 293, and on appeal at 41 ER 1171; *White v Dickson* (1881) 8 R 896). This right has been discussed in proprietary terms (*Caird v Sime* (1887) 14 R (HL) 37), and in pecuniary ones (*Cadell & Davies v Stewart*). In the *Cadell & Davies* case, an action to prevent publication of private letters between Robert Burns and a female friend, the pursuers' pleadings relied heavily upon property concepts and the notion of a continuing pecuniary right. In *Prince Albert v Strange*, the English case which provided the basis for the whole law of privacy protection in the United States of America, Vice-Chancellor Knight-Bruce talked of property in the thoughts and sentiments themselves (not merely the document in which they were recorded). Despite this comment, however, there may need to be some form of recording of the information to invoke control based upon property.

It may be, though, that it is not necessary to talk exclusively in property terms, whether in the information itself or the document in which it is recorded; for there is a group of cases under the heading of "common law copyright" (perhaps better described as the right to publicity) which suggests that the same kind of control over publication may be achieved by reference to a right to prevent publication of one's thoughts which is independent of ownership of their means of recording (if indeed recording is required). Because discussion of this right often occurs alongside (or as part of) property discussions, I shall also consider it here. In *White v Dickson* (1881) 8 R 896, for instance, which concerned an action by the relatives of a woman whose husband intended to publish private marital correspondence, it seems that their Lordships' discussion of the right to maintain literary privacy was not concerned with property arguments. The institutional writer Bell discusses the right in his *Principles* (1899: s.1357) and his *Commentaries* (1870: ii, 2,4,2,1), and concentrates very much on reputation as the basis for the right. The older Scottish authorities such as *Cadell & Davies* are more restrictive of the kinds of thought which may be protected and the requirement that they be recorded in some way, but extension by analogy, such as that achieved in *Prince Albert v Strange*, may be legitimate in this field.

Whether the above limited proprietary right and right to publicity are related aspects of a right to control personal information, or, as some cases suggest, independent of each other, it seems that both may provide protection for privacy. Where, for instance, private letters came into the hands of persons who were not intended to read them, the author should, on the above authorities, be able to prevent their publication. The situation as regards thoughts or sentiments not recorded in any form is more dubious, and the extent to which one may control information disclosed in such terms using the above principles is uncertain.

(ii) Privacy and moveable property

I mentioned in my discussion of the notion of privacy that one's property, as a social extension of the human being, can be seen as relevant to individual privacy. It suffices here to say on this point that if an individual infringes another's privacy by unlawfully removing or retaining his property, then that other may bring the action *rei vindicatio*, or restitution (in the property law sense), for the return of that property. This property remedy would only operate where property was removed. To remedy its mere examination *in situ* would require reference to some larger delictual principle of invasion of privacy, though if entrance had been unlawfully obtained to the locus of the property then the criminal law might have a role to play (as to which, see later).

(iii) Land ownership

The exclusive ownership of land brings with it a variety of rights, one of those being exclusive possession and use. This in turn generally entails a certain degree of privacy, for it enables one to be present on or in property, to the exclusion of all others. Anyone who threatens that privacy by, for instance, the wrongs of ejection or intrusion, may himself be subject to an action for summary ejection and damages, together with violent profits, so restoring the owner's privacy and sole occupation. Privacy can thus be seen as a component aspect or *right* in the wider collection of land rights. In Scots law, however, a certain caveat must be added. Where one has common ownership with another, and thus a certain, somewhat reduced state of privacy, but a degree of privacy nonetheless, the law will not prevent that other co-owner selling on his 50% pro indiviso share to 99 (or any other number of) others, thus diminishing greatly the degree of privacy which was enjoyed by the first co-owner. The law of land ownership thus provides no protection for the co-owner's limited privacy: his only option is to require division and sale of the land, which is his right. Only a sole owner enjoys the full privacy of *dominium* (and, even then, a superior's rights could affect this).

This caveat apart, the law does protect an individual's proprietorial rights in land through various doctrines, the utilisation of which can protect that privacy which I suggest is an aspect of landownership. The following make up aspects of this protection:

(a) Nuisance

The law of nuisance may provide some protection for privacy, principally against unwanted attention directed at an individual on his property (see generally Whitty 1988).

The scope of this area of the law concerns invasions of the interest of an occupier or landowner in his use and enjoyment of private land, and the interest of members of the public in the use and enjoyment of public places (Whitty 1988: para 2002). For the purposes of my discussion, it is the aspect of private land use and enjoyment which is most revealing.[4] There is a limitation, in that the nuisance-constituting activity must be of some permanence. It will normally be caused by a neighbouring landowner, but this is not exclusively so: the case of *Slater v A & J M'Lennan* 1924 SC 854 concerned a private nuisance caused by a road user to property he was passing, and *obiter dictum* in Baron Bernstein of *Leigh v Skyviews and General Limited* [1978] QB 479 suggested that surveillance by an aircraft might amount to a nuisance. Similarly, the telephone calls in the Khorasandjian case were presumably made from some distance away and perhaps not even on the defendant's property. In this case, the court found in favour of the plaintiff, who was the subject of harassment by the defendant's repeated telephoning of her, even though she was not a tenant or freeholder of the property. The case extends both the scope of nuisance-constituting activity which is actionable and also the class of litigant. There is scope then for utilising nuisance to defend the privacy of one's home and surrounding land even against those whose proximity to one's property is merely temporary.

An invasion of the interest in the use and enjoyment of land is only actionable in nuisance if the invasion is so unreasonable that the complainer should not have to tolerate it (Whitty 1988: para 2039). While physical damage is the main type of harmful conduct, it is clear that activities causing personal discomfort may constitute such conduct. Hence, spying on another's property may amount to an actionable nuisance as also now harassment by persistent telephoning.

The level of culpability of the defender is an issue of some debate: prior to the case of *RHM Bakeries (Scotland) Ltd v Strathclyde Regional Council* 1985 SLT 214, it had been thought that liability in nuisance was strict and not dependent on the fault of the wrongdoer. The ratio of this case, however, supports the proposition that there is no liability in nuisance unless culpa or fault is established, though the type of such (e.g. malice, intent, recklessness, negligence, and so forth) is left open (Whitty 1988: para 2087). Evidently, a strict liability nuisance law would favour the interest of the privacy-seeking pursuer, though the extent of the restriction imposed by this case has yet to be fully delineated.

The usual restrictions on the granting of interdicts mean that where the damage is complete and unless there is reasonable ground to apprehend a recurrence of it, an interdict cannot be granted (*Caledonian Railway Co v Glasgow & SW Railway Co* (1903) 11 SLT 510). Damages, however, would be available, though material damage, it has been observed, will be harder to show in the case of simple personal discomfort (Whitty 1988: para 2047). The public interest may operate to thwart the granting of interdict in nuisance cases also (*Forth Yacht Marines Ltd v Forth Road Bridge Joint Board* 1984 SLT 177), but it would be necessary to show that the land use itself was in the public interest (not, for instance, that the land use would provide a newspaper story which would be in the public interest).

(b) Planning decisions

In a similar way to the law of nuisance, whose concept of use and enjoyment of land is broad enough to employ the right to privacy as a barometer for measuring such enjoyment, cases involving planning proposals may involve consideration of privacy as a factor in arriving at the decision. This may be seen in *McMillan v Strathclyde Regional Council* 1984 SLT (Lands Trib) 25, which I have already mentioned (above, 4). In general, where an individual submits a planning application, "it is...a material consideration that a proposed development would result in loss of privacy" (Young and Rowan-Robinson 1985: 216) to his neighbour's property. While privacy is thus a valid interest to plead in planning cases, it is only of use to a neighbouring landowner. This is certainly a restriction, but the privacy of one's home is a major component of personal privacy, and the recognition of the interest in both the law of nuisance and planning indicate that it is protected as a consideration in Scots law.

(c) Trespass

The Scots civil law of trespass may provide a remedy against physical intrusion onto land. However, the usefulness of the action is severely restricted. Interdict is similarly restricted as in nuisance, and damages are not recoverable for bare trespass but only if actual damage has been suffered. While it is generally held to be a remedy incidental to the right of ownership, in several cases it has been actionable at the hands of a tenant (*Winans v Macrae* (1885) 12 R 1051; *MacLure v MacLure* 1911 SC 200). The extent to which one may take self-help action to remove a trespasser is unclear. Walker (1981: 939) is of the opinion that a trespasser may be ordered off the premises (this seems to amount to little more than asking someone to leave, which is hardly a remedy which needs stating), but not forcibly so unless he resists or threatens or does violence to the landowner or his property. His authorities on all these points are, however, very doubtful, though the cases of *Bell v Shand* (1870) 7 SLR 267 and *Wood v North British Railway* (1899) 2 F 1 provide firmer ground for the proposition that force may be used to remove an obstinate trepasser.

Clearly, loss is crucial to a remedy in trespass, as it is a requirement for damages, and an apprehension of loss is necessary for the granting of interdict. In many instances of privacy invasions, however, loss will be hard to show; it may simply be embarrassment, or annoyance, or having one's photograph taken (which was held in the English case of *Bernstein v Skyviews* [1978] QB 479 not to amount to trespass). For trespass to be more effective in remedying privacy invasions, a wider concept of loss would be required, or the action for damages would need, as in England, to be actionable without the need to show actual damage. The law in so many areas is tied to a notion of physical damage, an idea which hinders the protection of privacy.

VII: Criminal law

For many whose privacy is invaded, whereas utilising the civil law may be a long and uncertain process, the ability to telephone the police and have the privacy breacher swiftly dealt with under the criminal law might be very appealing. This is not to say that it should be principally by way of development of the criminal law that we should seek to provide greater protection for privacy; indeed, I will argue in the final section of this paper that we should be wary of any such development as the main plank in a reform of privacy law, and that such an avenue should be reserved for extreme cases. Existing avenues for privacy protection via the criminal law are limited, and they do not provide any redress of the wrong save through the punishment of the breacher of privacy by his conviction, compensation under the Criminal Injuries Compensation Scheme being restricted to victims of violent crime. Calcutt (1990) suggested therefore, in relation to the new offences proposed, that the victim should have the right to prevent publication of affected personal information, or, where publication had occurred, to damages and an account of profits.

(i) Criminal trespass

Civil trespass was mentioned above. The criminal law of trespass is found in the Trespass (Scotland) Act 1865, section 3 of which makes it an offence for anyone to lodge in any premises, or occupy or encamp on any land, being private property, without the consent of the owner or legal occupier. This envisages a degree of permanency which will not normally be present in an invasion of privacy, and is a major factor restricting the usefulness of this action.

(ii) Breach of the peace

Breach of the peace could potentially be used to cover privacy invasions. Indeed, high profile invasions, such as the besieging of an individual's home by the press, could, in extreme cases, constitute this offence. This is because breach of the peace is widely defined by the courts:

> There is no limit to the kind of conduct which may give rise to a charge of breach of the peace. All that is required is that there must be some conduct such as to excite the reasonable apprehension (that mischief may ensue) or such as to create disturbance and alarm to the lieges in fact (*Montgomery v McLeod* (1977 SLT (Notes) 77 per Lord Justice-General Emslie).

Furthermore, it has now been settled that a breach of the peace may occur in private. This means, for privacy protection, that where one is in a state of privacy, and this is disturbed by only one other individual, such conduct could in theory amount to a breach of the peace if within Lord Emslie's definition quoted above. Clearly, many invasions of privacy may cause alarm to individuals, particularly where the breacher persists in his or her conduct.

This having been said, I think we should be reticent in encouraging the use of breach of the peace as a means to provide redress for invasions of privacy. The offence already encroaches widely on civil liberties, and caution should be counselled in extending its application. It does have the merit, however, that it can be used in some cases to prevent anticipated mischief, and in this way provides the benefit (in the same way as interdict) most welcome in the eyes of the person whose privacy is at risk, of preventing an invasion of privacy before it occurs or, at least, becomes progressively worse.

(iii) Other offences

There may be scope for the utilisation of other offences in the protection of privacy: the Lord Chancellor's Department and the Scottish Office (1993) suggest the crime of fraud for example. The offences of theft by housebreaking or theft by opening lockfast places might also be appropriate in certain cases where items were removed. In utilising any criminal offences, however, the complainer is left to the mercy of the procurator fiscal, and many first-time offenders are merely faced with a caution. There is the point, too, that criminal charges do not entail that any information apprehended by the breacher can be kept out of circulation, unless they are stolen property. However, the use of the criminal law does at least provide swift action against privacy breakers, and transfers the economic burden of protecting the right of privacy (which as we have seen, can be regarded as part of the public interest) on to the public as a whole. Both Calcutt Reports suggested introducing new criminal offences as a way of tackling aspects of the privacy problem. I shall consider this extension of the criminal law in the final section of this paper.

VIII: Statute law

A few words on the use of statutes to protect privacy is required. Unlike other jurisdictions, there is as yet no statute in the United Kingdom which protects privacy in general. It is no doubt the case that one could point to minor provisions in many enactments which could be used to protect privacy; I leave detailed investigation to others. I should mention, however, two statutes which are of some importance for privacy, namely the Data Protection Act 1984 and the Interception of Communications Act 1985. Both of these have been much underused in protecting privacy, albeit there are restrictions on the protection they provide.

The Data Protection Act provides scope for protecting the *informational* aspect of privacy in that it requires those holding *personal data*[5] (in computerised form) to register with the statutory authority. Once registered, such data users are required to specify various aspects of the data they hold under an entry in the Register, and are thus subject to restrictions on the type of data they hold, its dissemination, the sources of the data, and so forth. Those seeking registration must comply with various principles set out in Schedule I: these include, notably, that information must be obtained fairly and lawfully. If such principles are derogated from, then under section 11 a deregistration notice may be served, and the data user will then be barred from holding personal data.

Clearly this Act could be of potential use against invasions of privacy by parties such as the media, as most newspaper stories are held on computer before they are sent to press. Such stories, if they contain personal information, will thus be covered by the Act. Not only, then, could a newspaper be subject to removal from the register of data users for breach of the data principles, but it could be liable in damages to the data subject for unauthorised disclosure of the data. It should be noted, however, that in respect of this right to compensation, it is authorisation by the data user and not the subject which is required to be absent, and that "distress" is only compensatable where it occurs along with damage, damage evidently being something more than mere hurt feelings. These two points restrict the right to claim damages. The threat of potential removal from the data register, a penalty which requires no need to show damage but merely breach of a data principle, remains however a weapon of some force against an infringing data user. It is a rather underused weapon, however, and it seems not to have been tried against newspapers, or professionals (such as doctors), holding personal information, where they have breached privacy. Statutory extension of data protection is forthcoming, as the European Community has been preparing for some time a Directive on Data Protection. This would extend data protection to manually recorded data also, a welcome step given that current protection of personal data in this form is only protected in certain cases (such as in the case of health records, under the Access to Medical Reports Act 1988), and would lay down as a general principle that personal data may be processed only if the data subject has consented to this.

As regards the Interception of Communications Act 1985, section 1 of this

Act makes it an offence intentionally to intercept a communication in the course of its transmission by means of a public telecommunications system, save in excepted cases. The cellular telephone operators' systems have now been included in the definition of public telecommunications systems. However, if the communication in question has left the public system, it is not covered by section 1. This applies to communications transmitted between telephone wall sockets and cordless telephones: these are not in the course of transmission by means of a public telecommunications system. Interception of such messages does not therefore contravene section 1 of the Act, as shown by the joined cases of *R v Effik and R v Mitchell* [1994] 3 All ER 458 (HL). Moreover, the offence only relates to interception: no further offence or remedy is provided for publication. The problem of publication is partly remediable, however, by section 5 of the Wireless Telegraphy Act 1949, which prohibits the disclosure of information as to the contents, sender or addressee of *any message* which is obtained using wireless telegraphy apparatus and would not otherwise have been obtained, as well as the use of such apparatus to obtain information as to such details. A useful exception applies to persons so acting with the permission of the Secretary of State or acting in the course of duty as a Crown servant. A fine at level 5 on the standard scale is prescribed for infringement. Interception, or disclosure of the contents (by wireless telegraphy equipment) of messages travelling between cellular base sets and handsets as well as cordless telephones and handsets is thus prohibited. The so-called metering of calls, that is recording the details of incoming and outcoming calls, would also seem to be caught, and thus, I believe, the publicised activities of the Lothian and Borders Constabulary in 1992.

Under the 1985 Act, whose prohibitions extend to communications transmitted by post also, an individual, suspicious of interception, can apply to a Tribunal to have the matter investigated. Quite apart from the limited remedies which are available to the Tribunal - discretionary compensation is available, but this is payable not by the offender, but by the Secretary of State - such an application presupposes knowledge on the part of the victim, which in many cases simply will not be the case. This, however, is a point concerning the sophistication of the means of intercepting communications, not a fault implicit in the Act.

Statutory protection of privacy does, thus, exist, but it is limited. Inherent in tackling the problems of invasion of privacy through statute is the requirement for a pursuer to bring his particular invasion within the exact wording and envisaged scenarios of the statute.

IX: The European Convention on Human Rights

The European Convention on Human Rights (ECHR) is of importance in providing basic principles of human rights which individuals are entitled to expect (mainly, though not exclusively, in their dealings with the state). Article 8 guarantees a right to respect for an individual's private and family life, as well as to his or her home and correspondence. This is a right which must be balanced against that in Article 10, which guarantees freedom of expression. However, the influence of the ECHR in Scots law is limited by the fact that the Convention is not part of the domestic law of Scotland, and individuals must rely on implementation of the findings of the European Court of Human Rights by the signatory states (of which the United Kingdom is one). For this reason, it is not proposed to say any more about this document, save that the commitment of the government in signing the document must be viewed as a precedent for a commitment to privacy protection.

Conclusion on the use of existing actions

I have indicated how existing law may be used to remedy invasions of privacy. The law does not, to any real extent, consider privacy an interest worthy of protection for its own sake, and the extent to which avenues in the law can be used to protect privacy, while greater than many would expect, and offering scope for intelligent litigants, is often arbitrary and unreasoned. The possibility of course exists of utilising several of the law's current remedies in conjunction. For instance, an action for breach of confidence could conceivably be raised in conjunction with a complaint to the police that the defender had also committed a breach of the peace. In any individual case, the victim of a breach of privacy would do well to consider the various possibilities which exist under the law in its present state. He may be lucky; he may not. Such is the capricious nature of the current protection of privacy offered by the law.

What is required is a commitment by the law to value privacy as an interest worthy of protection for itself, and thus to afford remedies for invasions of privacy *per se*, and means pre-emptively to avoid such invasions. How the law might achieve this is the question to which I now turn.

Development of legal remedies to protect personal privacy

The options for a greater commitment to privacy protection are various. Reform could be implemented via the criminal or the civil law, via statute or the common law, by taking legal measures or through extra-statutory bodies, by patching up the existing law, or else taking steps to provide a separate recognised action for breach of privacy.

(i) Criminal v civil law

Both Calcutt (1993) and the National Heritage Committee (1993) made recommendations as to the introduction of new criminal offences in respect of invasions of privacy. The National Heritage Committee, in most respects, merely reiterated the recommendations of Calcutt (1990), though noticeably removing the requirement that any of the offences should include the caveat "with a view to publication", to emphasise that the offences should apply to all citizens, not merely the media. Calcutt's recommendations applied only to

England and Wales; the National Heritage Committee extended this to Scotland also. I think that the reasons given for these proposals, namely, that the criminal law can react quickly, can provide prompt relief, and can act as a deterrent, are valid ones. However, I believe that the main thrust for breach of privacy protection should be made via the civil law. I am not convinced that the interest in privacy is of equal weight to that of physical integrity or liberty, save in extreme cases, such that the criminal law should be made to bear the principal, or even an equal, role in privacy protection. Balancing the competing civil rights of individual privacy and freedom of expression or speech is a difficult task for persons to undertake, and those who fall on the wrong side of the line should not necessarily be stigmatised with the penalties of the criminal law. However, certain flagrant breaches of privacy, constituted by clearly intended acts, are worthy of redress by the criminal law. The actions of those planting hidden surveillance devices or using them without knowledge, and those who intrude on others' physical seclusion or continually pester individuals, where no defence to their action can be realistically maintained, may be worthy of criminal sanctions. To the extent that the current criminal law does not provide redress, this may be an area for action. I would see this as secondary, however, to the main attack, which should come from the civil law.

(ii) Statute v common law

I have already noted the comment in Calcutt (1990) about the potential for common law development in Scotland of an action to protect privacy. This potential seems to have been neglected, however, and much of the discussion for progress now focuses on statute. A refusal to consider seriously development via the common law is lamentable, and indicates further the neglect of the subtleties of Scots law by the English legal and parliamentary establishment. Such a common law route is by its very nature more flexible than that of statute, and would allow the intricacies of a law protecting privacy to be developed over a considered period of time. Admittedly, though, initial uncertainty could be seen as a disadvantage by a potential litigant. However, it is to be hoped that test cases, in the wake of the first tentative steps in privacy protection revealed in *Henderson v Chief Constable of Fife* 1988 SLT 361, might be forthcoming. Perhaps the introduction of a similar procedure in Scotland to the Attorney General's Reference in England would be welcome in new or uncertain areas of the law such as this, to indicate the way forward. If the common law is to develop, it should do so recognising a right declared already inherent in Scots law. It should draw from the general principles of delict, and make provisions for the various defences required. It should be based upon the principle that a person whose privacy is infringed by physical access, information gained, attention paid to him, or interference with his personal property, to a level which would be considered by the reasonable person as unacceptable, should be entitled to redress for this.

On the other hand, statutory reform is able to offer a swift and certain means of addressing the problem, and any areas worthy of protection considered to have been omitted could be addressed through amendment (though parliamentary reform can often be slow and delayed). I would suggest that, if this approach is to be preferred (and it would appear that the government favours it), a general statement be provided for stating that invasion of personal privacy would be an actionable wrong, and that this statement be coupled with a non-limiting list of examples of actionable invasions. This would provide both a certain base for the action and also room for development of the limits of the action by the courts.

Whichever method is used, I would hope that the following points be taken on board:-

(a) Publication of any personal material gained by one who breaches privacy should not be required for the invasion to be actionable;

(b) Nominal damages should be available for mere invasions of privacy, with substantive damages available for patrimonial and sentimental loss, the latter increasing with the flagrancy of the infringement and the effect on the victim;

(c) Matters such as portraying the defender in a false light or publishing inaccurate or misleading information about him, should not *per se* be actionable under a privacy law, as they are conceptually different matters;

(d) Redress should be available for invasions caused intentionally, recklessly, or negligently: one's privacy protection should not be dependent upon the state of mind of the defender. Innocent infringement, however, in the absence of any element of fault, should not be remediable, but the innocent breacher should not be permitted to exploit his breach;

(e) Interdict should be available as a weapon to prevent invasions of privacy before they occur. Accounting of profits should, in appropriate cases, also be available, as should the remedy of delivery. I have already mentioned the question of damages;

(f) Defences of consent, lawful authority, and public interest would be required. The Lord Chancellor's Department and the Scottish Office (1993) suggested that there should be a defence of "information in the public domain" also. It is fair to say, however, that publicity accorded to something which has been previously reported or is only on a public register may still be seen as infringing privacy. Whether it should be actionable should depend upon the facts and the reasonable expectations of individuals.

(iii) The general law v statutory tribunals

Calcutt (1993) recommended the introduction of a statutory press tribunal, in the light of the failure of press self-regulation. Calcutt (1993: para 7.40) considered that this would acquire a "valuable expertise which is not generally available to the regular courts" and would be "more accessible". The National Heritage Committee (1993: para 39), *per contra*, were against such an idea. I would agree with the latter viewpoint, and with the argument that privacy measures should not just address the invasions of privacy perpetrated by the media, but should look at all invasions of privacy. An invasion of privacy by a neighbour, professional confidant, co-worker, or stranger may be equally offensive to the victim, and for the sake of conceptual coherence the problem should be tackled as a whole. For this reason, leaving matters to specialised statutory bodies dealing with particular professions is not a sufficient way to proceed. Nor would it be wise to provide for mirrored provisions in a press regulatory body as existed in a general law: there is no overwhelming reason why the press should be dealt with separately.

(iv) Shoring up the law v new remedies

From all that has been said above, it should be clear at this point that the law in its current form, while providing some means to redress privacy invasions, does not provide a coherent approach based upon an acceptance of the positive value of personal privacy. Furthermore, extending existing legal remedies would be insufficient, in that certain areas where action is required would still be poorly served, and the public commitment to privacy protection required by the law would be less highly evident. New ground needs to be broken.

Conclusion

The question of the legal protection of privacy concerns respect for the fundamental rights of human beings. Scots law has a strong tradition of providing redress to individuals for infringements of their basic interests, a tradition which dates back to the institutional writers and beyond. While the existing means of protecting personal privacy in the law must not be neglected, neither must we ignore the law's shortcomings in this area and the need for a specific commitment by it to protecting the fundamental right individuals have to privacy. This must, of course, be tempered by balancing the rights of others to freedom of speech and action. It is to be hoped that the current review of privacy being undertaken by the government will bring about such reform, with legal progress being based upon a proper understanding of the meaning and ambit of the concept of privacy. I am hopeful that this will be so, and that the very public discussion of the right to privacy which has been underway in legal circles in recent times will prove fruitful in moving the law in our country into line with that in so many others, by according legal recognition to a value universally acknowledged by societies as worthy of protection.

Property, Dignity, and the Human Body

Alexander McCall Smith

Synopsis

Upon what if any grounds is the law justified in taking action to limit an individual's freedom in relation to the use of the body? Three forms of activity may be considered in seeking to answer this question: sado-masochism for sexual gratification, sale of organs for transplantation, and surrogate motherhood. It is argued that the law may legitimately control such activities and limit individual autonomy in respect of them. The basis for this is the principle of dignity, which can be extended to the rejection of degradation and depersonalisation of another even where that other consents to the treatment involved. Some acts are in their essence not private, and interference with individual autonomy to prevent their occurrence is thereby justifiable.

* * * *

That we are entitled to do what we will with our bodies is, for many, a proposition that is no longer in doubt. The concept of autonomy - which performs an extraordinary range of labours in contemporary moral philosophy - holds that people are entitled to make decisions as to their fate without interference or hindrance from others, and that a life deprived of this freedom of self-disposition is a life deprived of authenticity. (See Haworth [1986] and Hill [1991]). Flowing from this, there has been broad, if sometimes grudging recognition of the right to engage in self-harming pursuits - to smoke, to drink to excess, to abuse drugs, and to engage in risky sexual practices. Not all of these are, in practice, universally acknowledged as rights, particularly where the private nature of the activity is doubtful (as in the case of drug use), but in much recent debate on this issue the onus appears to have been placed on those who would restrict such activities to justify what is seen as an unacceptable form of paternalism. For example, Husack (1992) makes a forceful philosophical argument for the moral right of adults to use drugs for recreational purposes. My aim here is to explore such justifications and to defend the view that there are grounds for using the law to prevent people from making certain uses of their body, or indeed, parts of their bodies. A great deal of freedom may be allowed in relation to the use of the body, but this freedom has certain limits, and in what follows an attempt will be made to delineate and justify such limits.

Three forms of activity will be considered: (1) the infliction of consensual physical harm for the purposes of sexual gratification; (2) the sale of organs for transplantation; and, finally, (3) the practice of surrogate motherhood. Each of these examples is particularly controversial, and attracts differing responses in various legal systems. Moreover, even where there is a clear legal response to the issue, the law may be out of kilter with an apparent liberal consensus on the matter. In the United Kingdom, for example, a substantial body of opinion accepts the legitimacy of all three of the above, and yet the law treats (1) and (2) as explicitly forbidden, while (3), although legal, is tolerated only within limits. This disparity of response is in itself interesting, although its sociological significance cannot be explored here.

Harming oneself

The libertarian position, which frowns on the exercise by the community of paternalistic measures, is based firmly on John Stuart Mill's renowned proposition that the only grounds upon which power may be exercised over an individual is to prevent his harming another. This view, which has perhaps been the dominant view in social philosophy during the second half of the twentieth century, has resulted in the firm rejection of any paternalistic measures intended to prevent people from harming themselves. In one of the best-known modern manifestations of this issue, the so-called Hart-Devlin debate (see Hart 1963; Devlin 1965), discussion has concentrated on such issues as prostitution and homosexual practices, with a clear majority of those participating coming down in favour of the Millsian position. More recently, Joel Feinberg (1988), a legal philosopher concerned with identifying the moral limits of the criminal law, has vigorously tested the liberal position and supported a highly non-interventionist ethic. This would now seem to be very much the *communis opinio*, and its acceptance amongst theorists has been reflected in an acknowledgment by legislators and by those concerned with the enforcement of the criminal law that matters such as adult homosexual conduct and prostitution in general are best left to the individual and are not a proper area of criminal law concern. The classical debate, then, appears to be largely over - at least in relation to the matters on which it traditionally focused. Some matters remain on the agenda, however - notably pornography. The difficulty here is one of classification: does pornography really involve harm to self or does it constitute a potential harm to others? The response of the feminist movement has been, to a considerable extent, to stress the harmfulness to women of pornographic imagery, an approach which takes it out of the private and places it firmly in the area of public concern.

Those who accept the libertarian position may have no difficulty in acknowledging that some conduct is unsettling - for example, masturbation, although almost universally practised, is something we do not necessarily like to *contemplate* - but they may nonetheless be adamant that such conduct is not a proper matter for social control or censure. This is likely to be because it simply causes no harm to anybody. Similarly, we may not find deviant sexual practices appealing - in fact, they may even disgust us - but this does not mean that we are harmed by the mere fact that such things are done. It may be that we find the idea of three people engaged simultaneously in sexual intercourse to be distasteful; it may be that we find repellent the very notion of more extreme perversions, such as coprophilia, and yet it is difficult to locate in such activities anything which we could reasonably describe as harm.

At the next level there is conduct which is harmful in that at least *some* harm occurs, but this is harm which is of such a nature as to justify intervention. Promiscuous sexual activity may involve harm of this sort. A man who deliberately seduces his partners and then abandons them after a short time may cause considerable emotional harm to his victims, who may have had a very different view of their involvement. This is harm, just as the consequences of adultery may be harmful. Distress is caused, and this distress may be as painful as the harm suffered by the victim of a physical assault. We punish assault, and yet we do not punish adultery. Why? One possible explanation is that we are dealing here with an interest which cannot be protected in a way which is compatible with a reasonable degree of social freedom. Such harms are an inevitable result of living in society and engaging with others; we must expect some emotional disappointments - even emotional disaster. Such harm is also possibly seen as consensual. By entering into emotional relationships with others, we implicitly consent to the risk of rejection. We therefore cannot blame anybody for this harm; we assume the risk of it the moment we engage with others.

Consent is an important feature of these private harms. If we agree to submit ourselves to harm, it ceases to be a matter of intervention because its infliction does not infringe our autonomy in any way. The very act of consenting to a risk constitutes an exercise of our autonomy; it is what we want for ourselves, and in choosing it we implicitly indicate that we are not being wronged. We would, in fact, feel a keener sense of wrong if we were prevented from submitting to the apparent harm. The protective parent who seeks to prevent an adolescent from entering upon an emotional adventure because he foresees that it will result in a distressing let-down infringes the autonomy of his child and does him a wrong.

Not all harm, then, constitutes a wrong to another. Harm to self affects nobody but the person who agrees to undergo it, or the risk of it, and in doing so does no more than exercise his autonomy. For the libertarian then, harm to self is qualitatively different from harm to others in that it involves no wrong; doing something which sets back *your own interests* is a quite permissible form of conduct. Not everybody would accept this, of course. In some religious traditions, the self is conceived of as an entity which can be wronged even by the individual who constitutes that self. Thus in certain varieties of religious doctrine suicide is traditionally seen as wrong because it involves an act of disposal over that which is a divine gift and which may not, therefore, be rejected by the recipient. This view, which sometimes forbids lesser harms, including self-mutilation of the body for whatever motive (such as vasectomy), depends on a teleological vision of the self which is antipathetic to contemporary notions of self-determination and individual autonomy, and is difficult to justify outside its very specific theological framework. Yet even if the self is not seen as the creation of some "other" to whom a duty of husbandry is owed, it may still be the subject of duties on the part of the individual. This is so in Kantian theory, where the duty which one owes to oneself is grounded upon the proposition that conduct towards oneself may be generalised, and that causing harm to *n* is wrong, even if *n* happens to be the agent himself. In this view, self-harm may become a wrong, and therefore intervention to prevent it is not, strictly speaking, paternalistic at all.

It may be possible to construct grounds for the wrongfulness of harming oneself, even when no other person is affected by one's action, but an alternative, less controversial approach is possible. This involves locating in some forms of apparently harmless conduct an actual or potential harm to others, and justifying legal regulation on these grounds. In other words, the issue is raised as to how many of the instances of alleged harm to self are in fact truly cases of harm to self. In particular, is it possible to detect harm to others in the three areas under scrutiny? If it is, then intervention to prevent or regulate them can no longer be seen as paternalistic and the liberal case against intervention in such cases is seriously weakened. We might turn, then, to our three cases to see whether these are indeed cases where the freedom of the individual to do as he wishes with his body may properly be subjected to limit.

Consensual physical harm

There are many forms of harm which, if inflicted consensually, are of no interest to society and do not attract the attention of the criminal law. Many contact sports are in this category; boxing and wrestling, if performed within the rules, are quite legal, as are other pastimes, such as sky-diving, which may involve a considerable risk of harm to the participant. The criminal courts have ruled from time to time that risky entertainments are not criminal, provided they keep to the rules (see, for example, *Attorney-General's Reference (No.6 of 1980)* [1981] 2 All ER 1057). It is also legal to submit to procedures such as ear-piercing, tattooing, or male circumcision, although these all involve a degree of harm to the body.

Such harms might be treated as acceptable because it is considered that they involve negligible damage, or because the damage which they do is felt to be damage of a sort which the individual may properly choose to inflict on himself. The first of these is readily understandable; we simply need not concern ourselves with minor matters. The second, however, is more complex, and takes us to the heart of the tolerance issue. Why should some forms of self-harm be acceptable while others should not? At first glance, the distinction seems to be one of degree - minor harms are acceptable, major ones are not - but this hardly provides an answer which is satisfactory in principle. There must be some basis for distinguishing between the minor injury involved in, say, ear-piercing, and the major injury involved in the severing of a limb. If there is no difference in principle, then it is difficult to see why we should allow, say, the body blow of boxing, and not allow the sword thrusts of gladiatorial combat.

This issue arose recently in a controversial English criminal case, *R v Brown*

[1992] 2 WLR 441 in which a number of sado-masochists were convicted of assaulting one another. The acts which formed the basis of the charge were extremely sadistic, and included the nailing of genitals to boards and the infliction of a variety of other injuries -but they were all consented to by the participants and nobody died. The defence appealed the convictions up to the House of Lords, which eventually decided by a majority to uphold conviction, in the face of vigorous argument on the consent point. The argument was, in fact, even more vigorous outside the court, with outraged protest against the decision being made by homosexual activists and by some civil liberties groups. The consensual infliction of violence in this case was seen as something with which the courts simply had no business to interfere. The relevant Scottish decision, which involves a non-sexual, consensual physical assault (a 'square go') is *Smart v HM Advocate* 1975 SLT 65, in which the court held that a consensual assault was a criminal offence on the grounds that there was *wicked intent*.

There is clearly narrow legal justification, in terms of the precedents, for the decision which was reached in *Brown* but it is the policy implications which are more troublesome. The decision has few friends in this respect - at least in the press and among commentators - and it must be acknowledged that in so far as it attempts any degree of legal regulation of sexual behaviour it is swimming against a very strong tide of opinion, including that of the Law Commission, the official body charged with the reform of all branches of English law. Yet there is one respect in which the decision can be defended, namely, that it affirms the moral significance of the human body, and consequently that it asserts certain values which are essential to civil society.

The defence of this position must start with murder. The taking of human life, other than in self-defence, meets with virtually universal condemnation. The reasons for this disapproval may be located in a variety of elaborated moral positions, but they are also intuitive. We do not approve of killing because it offends our respect for the principle of *vitality*, a notion which provides a justification for the prohibition against killing which is quite independent of any argument that killing is wrong because it deprives the victim of his right to life (Kleinig 1991).

This independence of any rights argument is important because it means that consensual killing is wrong too. The fact that a person asks to be killed does not make the killing morally acceptable, even if it may mitigate it slightly. Certainly, in the legal context, it has never been a defence for a person accused of murder to say that the victim agreed or asked to be killed. In this respect the law has done no more than embody the strong moral conviction that the principle or respect for vitality is one that admits of no exceptions, at least in so far as human life is concerned.

If the principle of respect for vitality is accepted, then we might test its extrapolation from killing to cover the implications of less serious forms of physical harm. Some extension would seem relatively uncontroversial, particularly in those cases where life is put at risk by conduct which is so risky that it poses a serious risk that life will be lost. Here the risky conduct can probably be condemned on the same grounds as we condemn killing. The playing of

Russian roulette, therefore, is wrong for the same reason that it is wrong to aim a loaded weapon at another and deliberately pull the trigger. As conduct becomes less risky, though, it becomes increasingly difficult to justify its condemnation on vitality grounds. There is always a risk that virtually any sport could result in death, but we do not condemn sport on grounds of risk to life - the risk is acceptable, because it is remote and also because the participants do not demonstrate any contempt for human life by participating in the sport.

It would be quite inconsistent with our general position to say that the sado-masochistic activities in the *Brown* case are to be condemned purely on the grounds that they involved a slight risk to life. There is, however, a challenge to human dignity here, and it is in respect of the implications of such conduct for human dignity that the reason for moral objection can be found. The principle of respect for human dignity protects the human body from certain forms of degrading treatment - such as torture - which are, in the usual case, something *inflicted upon* an unwilling sufferer. Yet human dignity is arguably a broad enough concept to protect those whose degradation is consensual. A degrading act affects not only the individual human being upon whom it is inflicted, but human beings in general *if there is no response to it on the part of the community*. The torturer, therefore, does more than inflict pain on his victim, he contradicts human values in general; if the state fails to condemn what he does, it makes a statement about his view of humanity, and of human dignity, which is capable of being generalised beyond the immediate context; in contemplating the degradation of another human being, we see a diminution of the human being. Witnessing this may, of course, lead to renewed determination to protect the values which are thereby threatened; indeed our outrage at cruelty or torture may be strengthened by our direct experience of it. But what if our outrage is denied - if we are told that what we see is not outrageous at all, but quite acceptable? In such circumstances, we are, quite simply, confused, even brutalised. We cease to care about it. For this reason, alone, it is wrong to make light of insults to human dignity, even if these insults take place within the framework of a willing victim. Even if it were the case that consent means that there is no harm caused to an individual, there is real harm caused to our moral sensibilities by the portrayal of violence, even by actors, if the portrayal of cruelty is done casually or, does not take place within a morally acceptable framework (that is, one which portrays cruelty as wrong). A consequence of abandoning this framework can be a moral numbness, in which we simply do not react to human cruelty because we do not experience any distress over it.

The notion that the human body has some form of symbolic significance which is capable of being weakened in this way is at work, too, in our attitudes towards the dead. The dead are beyond the experience of pain or humiliation, and yet we do not tolerate acts calculated to degrade their human remains (May 1972; Tindale 1992). No morally sensitive community would allow the subjection of a dead body to public insult, for example, by allowing the drawing and quartering of the bodies of executed criminals. Such a practice strikes us as barbaric, not because any harm can come to the dead themselves, but because we see in such treatment an attitude of profound disrespect towards the dignity of every individual.

The sceptic may argue at this point that this is placing excessive store by the human body, which frankly does not have (or no longer has) the significance which is being suggested for it. There is some force to this objection; attitudes towards the human body undoubtedly change. The concept of nobility in the human form - expressive of rationality and of beauty - may have been the artistic ideal of the Renaissance, but to artists of our own times the human body is a much more day-to-day functional entity. The human form today is seen in a much more mechanistic light and is hardly invested with any transcendent quality. There are few tabus on nudity in western society, and certainly there are few who will experience disquiet over the portrayal of nudity. The naked body may still have a sexual significance, but it seems to have little romantic or moral significance. The human body, in short, has largely been demystified.

The fact, though, that this change in attitude has occurred may point to an important moral shift. If the human body is "demystified" in this way, then the moral nature of the relationship with the body may change. The difference may be crucial; if we look at a picture of the victims of war strewn about a roadside, what do we feel? We should feel outrage at the large-scale abrupt ending of a series of human lives - at the ending of the ordinary human hopes and ambitions embodied in these remains. But what the brutalised eye, the eye accustomed to the view that there is nothing particularly shocking about mutilated bodies, sees may be just that, and nothing more - ordinary, human bodies. The emotional impact is weakened and it becomes so much easier for us to accept that which should be unacceptable. And for some, at least, it becomes so much easier, too, to *do* the unacceptable.

Of course, all of this may be accepted by the libertarian, who might respond that this argument does nothing more than justify a ban on the public portrayal of torture or cruelty. From this perspective, the prohibition of private, con-sensual acts of torture will do nothing to achieve the protection of the values which such intervention seeks to protect. This is to ignore, though, the expressive function of the law. The criminal law is one of the few remaining vehicles for the public expression of morality, and even if it is going to make little difference as to how people in fact conduct themselves, at least the *Brown* decision makes it clear that such conduct is wrong. Those then who take any moral bearings from what is licensed or forbidden by the criminal law - and it is at least arguable that the criminal law in this respect has an educational role - will be left in no doubt by this decision as to what the moral value of the human body is.

The sales of organs

Self-harm of the sort involved in the *Brown* case is not an everyday problem; by contrast, the question of how we are to make available more human organs for transplantation purposes is a matter of practical concern for a considerable number of people enduring daily discomfort. The issue of control over the human body arises here too, both in relation to "opting out" systems for the removal of organs from fresh cadavers (without requiring advance consent or the consent of relatives) and also in respect of the question of whether people should be entitled to sell a kidney of their own to those in need of a transplant.

There is widespread agreement that the method by which the transplantation of organs is currently regulated in the United Kingdom is defective and that, as a result, the supply of organs for transplantation purposes is inadequate (Mason and McCall Smith 1993: 291). A major difficulty lies in the securing of the necessary consent of relatives once a suitable donor is found, consent which is sought even when the donor has expressed an advance wish to donate an organ. Under an opting-out system, which is applied in a number of countries, including a number of western European countries, it is possible for doctors to remove organs unless the patient has registered his name in advance on a list of objectors. This system appears to result in many more organs being made available than under the British system. In Belgium, for example, the introduction of opting out legislation led to a doubling of the rate of transplants within a year of the legislation's coming into force (Bos 1991 : 69)

It is probably the case that an opting-out system would lead to considerable improvements in the supply of fresh organs; but even if such a system were introduced, the question would still remain as to whether a market in human organs should be allowed to exist alongside a system of implicit or explicit donation. From a practical point of view, there would be scope for such a market, as the availability of a suitable organ from a dead donor is a fairly haphazard matter. A living donor, by contrast, may be identified more easily and advance arrangements made. In practice, such markets have grown up in a number of countries, and it was the discovery in January 1989 that a discreet one existed in London that led to the passage of emergency legislation in the United Kingdom to outlaw the practice of paying for organs. The statute which was passed to deal with this matter - the Human Organ Transplantation Act of 1989 - makes it a criminal offence to advertise a human organ for transplantation purposes or to advertise for a donor. It is also an offence under this act for any person to remove an organ from a living donor, unless there is a genetic relationship between the parties or approval for the transplantation is obtained from the Unrelated Live Transplant Regulatory Authority.

The refusal of Parliament to countenance the sale of organs reflects a very broad antipathy to this process, which has been condemned at both national and international level. Not only have individual governments acted to prevent the practice but the World Health Organisation has made it clear that it regards the selling of organs as an affront to the most basic human values. Yet there are those who see this as an intolerable interference in liberty of choice and the right of self-disposal. Although the context is very different, the issue of principle is perhaps the same as that which might be raised by the opponents of the *Brown* decision. Why should people be prevented from dealing with their bodies in the way which they see fit? Why should you not be able to do with your kidneys whatever you will, particularly if a result of your action will be to relieve the suffering of another? Again, the simple, insistent self-determination point is not easy to refute, and even if there is an intuitive conviction that the sale of organs is wrong, formulating a satisfactory basis for this moral conviction is not simple.

One of the most forceful recent statements of the case for the allowing of a market in human organs is that put forward by the philosopher John Harris (1992), who starts off with what he describes as an instinctive aversion for the notion of commerce in body parts but concludes his analysis of the issue by holding that such a market has an important role to play in the provision of organs for transplantation. (See also Perry 1980; Brams 1977.) Harris directly confronts the notion that the sale of organs amounts to an improper *use* made of the donor. It is not wrong, he suggests, to make use of people; we do it all the time in engaging others to render services - in some cases, services which they would rather not have to render. Use of others becomes wrong, of course, if it amounts to exploitation. Exploitation, however, involves the taking of something from another for an inadequate reward, or using some form of coercion or improper pressure to do so; only if these features are present can a transaction be called exploitative. Even then, in an economically unjust and imperfect world, Harris has doubts about whether we should prevent the poor from using what means they have to better their financial position, even if this does involve their being exploited by others.

The focus which Harris chooses is what might be termed the "justice" of the exchange between the parties. This leads him into an economic view of the matter, with a strong consequentialist emphasis. The determining consideration in his view is whether there are benefits in an organ market which outweigh concerns as to its moral doubtfulness, and in his view this is in fact the case. If there is some harm to the seller, then that harm is almost always going to be overshadowed by the good which the act of donation achieves. This does not mean, of course, that one completely discounts any harm which the sale of organs may entail; it is just that the harm is, quite simply, worth incurring on utilitarian grounds.

In complete contrast to this view, many philosophers who are opposed to a market in bodily parts rely on a dignity-based, Kantian approach, arguing that the very fact of the sale of a body part constitutes a commercialisation of the body, and therefore compromises the dignity of the individual (Chadwick 1989). In some cases, matters are left there, without further explanation, but in recent notable contributions to the debate an attempt is made to explain just how a Kantian rejection of commercialisation can be justified. In essence, the argument is that to allow the body to be seen as an object of commerce means that it becomes a *thing*, and that the distinction between persons and things is thereby weakened (Munzer 1994). Persons are worthy of respect - they are, in Kantian terms, part of the kingdom of ends, and each of them has equal value. Things, by contrast, may be used without thought; one may sell a thing, abuse it, and even destroy it, and in so doing no harm is done. The distinction between the moral status of a thing and a person could hardly be more marked.

Slavery is a supreme insult to the value of persons. The slave is a thing - he is within the scope of commercial dealing - and the assault on his dignity is complete. In practice, the lot of the slave may be relatively comfortable - he may want for little and may enjoy considerable privileges. Yet we would probably be inclined to hold that the sheer fact that he can be bought and sold amounts to a major wrong to him, even if he consents to a contract of slavery. This position is sometimes justified on the grounds that his autonomy is taken from him by his slavery, and that a deprivation of autonomy is something which the doctrine of autonomy itself cannot permit. This, however, is inadequate; there are many ways in which we may limit our autonomy in ways which are quite acceptable, largely because these arrangements do not necessarily completely deny our dignity. It is the fact of property itself which makes the difference - the *reification* of the human which so offends our fundamental notions of what it is to be a person.

This objection is very similar in nature to the objection identified in the discussion of consensual violence. In that context, human dignity is compromised because of the cruelty offered to the body (which represents the human). In the case of organ sales, the body is similarly degraded to the status of a thing that can be used for ends independent of the body. The body is therefore *depersonalised*, and this, for the same reasons as in the case of the infliction of violence, detracts from the moral status of the human body in general.

It will be clear that this approach need not necessarily be paternalistic. Although there may be those who would see the prohibition of the organ market as being intended to protect people from degrading their own dignity, the justification advanced above focuses on the implications for the community as a whole of any diminution of human dignity. The protection of human dignity promises very clear and definite goods for the community; these are threatened if human dignity is compromised, and this indeed is a consequentialist consideration which might possibly enter into the utilitarian calculations proposed by Harris. In other words, the good of the greater availability of organs may be realised, but at the same time we run the risk of further demeaning individual dignity and human worth as the process of slow blunting, or numbing, of our moral sensibilities proceeds.

Why should sale of an organ compromise human dignity while the donation of an organ does not? It is perhaps too easy to respond glibly that money corrupts, without explaining why it should have this effect. Yet there is clearly at work here some intuition to the effect that the involvement of money in one case and the absence of money in the other make the two cases morally distinct. In fact, the theoretical grounds for distinction are fairly strong. The person who gives an organ does not treat his body as a thing within the ambit of commerce; whereas the seller of an organ does. The donation is therefore an act of altruism which is thoroughly consistent with ideals of human dignity; it is as far away from slavery as it is possible to be.

Surrogate motherhood: the womb as an object of commerce

In a transaction of commercial motherhood we encounter another question of the legitimacy of markets. In many countries commercial surrogacy is either an outlawed transaction or it is illegal to do anything to facilitate the implementation of such a contract. The latter opinion is the one which is embodied in the United Kingdom legislation on the subject, the Surrogacy Arrangements Act 1985 which makes no attempt to prohibit private surrogacy arrangements entered into by individuals but which criminalises the advertising of surrogacy services or the taking of reward for facilitating a surrogacy arrangement.

The British legislation has been widely criticised, once again on the grounds that it sets out to restrict the exercise of a right of bodily self-determination while, at the same time, preventing an arrangement which can in theory lead to the pleasure and fulfilment of all those involved. The surrogate mother is paid her fee; the commissioning parents get a child; and the child gets a loving home. Of course things may go wrong, and do, and there may be disputes over the custody of the child, but it could be argued that this may be laid in great measure at the law's door for failing to provide an adequate legal framework for the proper regulation of surrogate arrangements.

The main objection to surrogacy lies perhaps in the fact that the body is, as in our other two examples, used in a way which offends its dignity. The surrogate surrenders, for the use of others, a function which is essentially linked with the most intimate aspects of human life, an aspect potentially charged with more emotion and significance than any other human activity. In this respect, the surrogate and the prostitute are not entirely dissimilar; both allow themselves to be used by another for a purpose which will abstract from the activity which is most personal to them. The prostitute degrades the whole significance of human sexual congress, not for herself, but for all; the surrogate degrades the concept of motherhood by indicating that it means nothing to her to abandon the child whom she has conceived. This is the real objection to both. The body becomes a thing, an object of sale, and the child, ultimately, is bought.

Conclusion

The argument that has been presented here, if accepted, can paint its proponents into an apparently illiberal corner in which a somewhat perfectionist view of human nature would press us to condemn a number of apparently "private" acts. It is a central thrust of the argument, though, that these acts *are not private*, and that we need constantly to monitor the creeping expansion of the realm of the private. In particular, we must be careful to ensure that moral numbness does not follow from the development of the view that what people do with their own lives is of no concern to the community in general (see George 1993). This highly individualistic approach is fundamentally antipathetic to any real notion of community, and must lead ultimately to a moral desert. The communitarian, who rejects his vision of a society of pervasive moral pluralism, will argue that moral pronouncements of a general nature have to be made by the agencies of the state (such as the criminal law) if any community of moral values is to exist. Without these guidelines, the creation of a community of values is impossible, with self-evidently distressing results. We must be able to assume that those with whom we share our lives share at least some common values, including, as a very minimum, a level of respect for human dignity. Law is one of the ways in which these common values are expressed. People look to the courts for justice, for the assertion of right and wrong. If the courts cannot provide that, then people feel angry and bereft. One might hope that the criminal law will be tolerant, but one cannot expect it to be morally relativistic.

It is a further implication of the argument that the expansion of the realm of the commercial is inherently threatening to the concept of human dignity. If we all have our price, then what room is there left for other values? If we reduce all our dealings with one another to a matter of currency, then we may end up measuring human worth in monetary terms. If we deny the duty of succour and charity and reduce medical care to the payment by the patient for the services of the doctor, then we weaken the human imperative to care for and protect the vulnerable.

Contemplating torture and failing to condemn it; selling organs; and hiring out the body (either the womb or the sexual organs) all reduce the inherent dignity of the human body. It may be that the legislature and the courts cannot stop any of these things being done, but they must be seen to make a statement which shows that the value of human dignity, as inextricably linked with the view that the human body is not to be trivialised, is recognised and protected.

Scientific Research and Intellectual Property

W R Cornish

Synopsis

Academic and publicly funded research institutions are currently much concerned with intellectual property rights. This is connected with the drive to capitalise commercially upon basic research, and gives rise to issues about the scope of intellectual property, particularly patents. These issues are especially acute in the fields of biotechnology and the patentability of life, notably the human genome. Questions have also arisen about the introduction of second-tier or "utility model" protection in the United Kingdom, and the conflict between the academic desire to publish for peer esteem and the industrial/commercial prefer-ence to seek a competitive lead through the preservation of secrecy. Finally, there has been debate over the extent to which moral issues should be incorporated within patent law and, if allowed, who should be charged with decision-making in these areas. The paper concludes that the development of intellectual property rights in relation to academic research, and the resultant commercialisation of that research, should be supported but must avoid hostility and protest as far as possible. There is a need for education in the nature of intellectual property and its place in the conversion of scientific knowledge to commercial account.

* * * *

Introduction

It is both flattering and enjoyable to be invited to come north in order to deliver the 1994 Miller Lecture. Fortunately my subject is not one which gives rise to cross-border difficulties. The law of intellectual property in the United King-dom can for most purposes be regarded as British law; indeed it is showing signs of becoming European Union law more rapidly than any other branch of commercial law.

The campuses and the academic research institutions of this country, as so many others, are suddenly seized with concern over intellectual property rights - IPRs - and a sense of profound unease about them. There are numerous points at which some form of IP - be it patents, protected secrets, copyright, plant variety rights, semi-conductor chip rights or whatever - have an increased or indeed novel significance for activities in the academic sphere. Thanks to the current electronic and biotechnological revolutions the impact on the natural sciences is daily increasing. I cannot attempt to talk about all the ramifications in a single lecture. My prime focus will be upon the most crucial of IPRs - patents for inventions.

The view that this country has admirable science but fails dismally to capitalise on its technological propensities is often enough heard. The same regret is voiced in other countries, but it probably applies to us in particular. We have blamed it above all on a failure to build upon the theoretical and structural work, designated basic research, which in large measure is undertaken in the public sector - in the universities and in publicly funded research establishments.

Until recently, the overall climate did not favour doing much about the situation. Academic scientists valued their freedom to choose their subjects for research, and they found the challenges of basic theory more enticing and more rewarding than the working out of practical applications. Their choices might be conditioned by the need for research funding outside ordinary departmental budgets, in which case they would have to persuade research councils, charitable foundations or industrial sponsors of the value of their proposals. But by and large they set their own agenda. They looked to peer approval for recognition, sometimes adopting a hostile, and more often an indifferent, attitude to the commercialisation of results.

It was appreciated, whether from hard experience or remoter observation, that the path from some initial breakthrough in perception or knowledge, which counts as "invention", to the production of goods and processes on a commercial scale, is mostly long and hard. It will generally need to be supported by venture capital in some form and by other types of initiative and know-how. It is not a track down which an academic researcher is likely to be drawn personally, so long as he chooses not to spin himself off completely into industrial activity.

In the past, therefore, when the initial research developed around funding from industry, or joint collaboration on the work, the usual arrangement (sometimes it was only an unvoiced assumption) was that the industrial partner's main return would consist in taking up the commercial prospects for itself. There would often be, for instance, a clause in the terms of collaboration giving all resulting IPRs to it.

If the research came from specific government funding, then rights of exploitation would pass, as a condition of the grant, to the National Research Development Corporation, set up for just this purpose after the Second World War. Certainly this exclusive arrangement was not without its merits. The NRDC made considerable sums, notably out of its cephalosporin patents, and passed back part of the royalties earned to the inventors and their institutions. But the organisation was criticised by some for a remoteness which left too much to be initiated by the researchers.

It was only in the cases of charity funding and research done without special assistance that an academic scientist was free to act as he chose over the exploitation of results. Even then there were obscurities on the issue of whether he or his institution owned the patents and other IPRs in the research. It was indicative of the culture that the legal question was not definitively settled. In universities the matter has come to be regulated now in terms of employment, mainly because the Patents Act 1977 for the first time introduced a statutory definition of the circumstances in which employees hold initial rights for their employers. Certainly the Committee of Vice-Chancellors and Principals has taken this statutory formulation to mean that universities now own patents granted on their academics' research; and most universities state this expressly in their rules governing employment, while at the same time fixing shares in IP royalties by a division scheme between inventor, university and (in many cases) department (Cornish 1992).

This interest in explicit arrangements for IPRs is one indicator of a new determination not to let the commercial potential of academic research disappear through neglect. It stands alongside various other shifts:

First, there is much greater interest on the part of government in the development of joint research initiatives between universities and one or more industrial partners, through schemes such as LINK, a movement destined to be intensified by involvement of the Research Councils as the plan proposed in the Cabinet Office paper, *Realising Our Potential* (1993), is carried through into the Technology Foresight Programme. Widespread contacts between scientists and businessmen are currently being organised through that Programme, which is to have a considerable influence on the allocation of public research funds in the science base.

Secondly, there has been the conversion of the NRDC in the early 1980s into the British Technology Group (BTG) and then, following a similar US move, the ending of its monopoly over exploitation of government-funded research results. This has put universities into a position where they can choose for themselves how to go about a good deal of exploitation; moreover the BTG has now been fully privatised into a keen-eyed entrepreneur with a good deal of know-how across the industrial spectrum; not only does it now have a branch in the US but the beginnings of a European arm through technology transfer offices in continental universities. At the same time its loss of position as a government-sponsored institution may be signalling, particularly to foreign competitors, that there is no longer the same determination to back patents in university inventions in the harsh conditions of the market-place.

Thirdly, in universities old and new, and in research institutes, special offices have been set up, which to begin with dealt primarily in "industrial liaison" - the organisation of links with industry on joint research - but which are coming now to be concerned with "technology transfer" - the uncovering of exploitable ideas and the acquisition and deployment of IPRs in them. This is a movement much favoured by government, as is evidenced by the Cabinet Office paper, *Intellectual Property and the Public Sector Research Base* (1992). The DTI has made special funds available for technology audits and is full of plans for strengthening and diversifying the Technology Transfer Units so that they have appropriate connections with the outside world of venture capital, IP acquisition and technology licensing expertise. Obviously there are great differences in type and scale of opportunities from one campus to another.

The first object of an active TTU is to be on site and readily accessible. It can then raise awareness of commercialisation prospects among research staff - and indeed in the student community as well. It can review particular prospects and keep up active planning. It can reach adequate agreements with industrial sponsors; or where there are no such arrangements, it can secure IP protection, encourage further work needed to expand that protection, and then bring the whole to a firm stage where there can be hard-nosed discussions with one or more industrial exploiters. This last form of activity grows from an understanding that patents for inventions are only of value if they are in broad enough terms to prevent competitors from introducing novelties that are similar but not identical to the invention actually made. This requires a sophisticated appreciation both of the problems which may arise from earlier publications and of the need to persuade patent offices to grant a patent specification with sufficiently broad claims to protection. This may well call for additional research to be undertaken which is directed primarily at supporting the eventual patent or patents. Only by such strategic activity, extending perhaps over years, can a university expect to be treated seriously in a commercial world.

The scope of patent systems

Against this background, I turn to questions of the range and effectiveness of IPRs, with particular emphasis on patent systems. For those unfamiliar with their basic form, may I note three major characteristics of patents which are crucial to an understanding of what I want to say.

First, like other forms of IPR, the rights are granted by states for their own territories. Accordingly, international coverage for a single invention can be secured only on a country-by-country basis.

Secondly, patents, being rights which are good in law against the whole world, including even an independent inventor of the same concept, must be the subject of an application to a patent-granting office for the country in question. Today, in many advanced countries, an application will only blossom into a patent after an official search of the technical literature and examination on the results of that search, in order to determine that the invention qualifies for protection.

Thirdly, steps have been taken to eliminate some of the duplication involved in securing patents across a range of countries. The Patent Cooperation Treaty (1970) provides for an international search, and to some extent for international examinations, in contracting states around the world. National authorities retain the final power to determine what shall be granted for their own territories. The European Patent Convention (1973) has established a European Patent Office (EPO), with headquarters in Munich. It provides an alternative route to the various national patent offices by which to apply for patents in European states. Through a single application, the EPO may grant of a bundle of similar patents for such of those states as are designated in the application. It was part of this European alternative that the basic principles of validity and infringement of patents were standardised in all the collaborating states. This European concordat, which has been in operation since 1978, sets the whole shape of patenting in the EEA and beyond. Future reforms thus depend to a considerable extent upon securing the assent of the large number of states involved, and will accordingly be difficult to bring about.

Over the last half-century, the scope of patent systems has advanced a short step behind new technologies. In particular, the chemical revolutions in agriculture and pharmaceuticals, including production by microbiological techniques, have sparked legal expansion. At some stage most industrial countries have abandoned earlier barriers, such as prohibitions on the patenting of chemical substances, or of pharmaceuticals, or restrictions which allowed patents for chemicals only when produced by a particular method. While old bans on the patenting of methods of treating humans (and in some countries, treating animals as well) have mostly remained in place, they have been confined to procedures for conducting surgery and diagnosis. The embargo has been very substantially by-passed: in the European concordat, for instance, it does not apply to the patenting of new substances, or substances with new therapeutic and other medical uses (EPC Art 52(4); cf Art 54(5); *Eisai's Application* [1987] OJ EPO 147).

These expansions of patent systems have been significant enough to affect the very structure of industries. Those in universities who conduct research which has fed in to those industries have accordingly been able to draw their part-share from this development. Had it not taken place, there would be comparatively little interest now in the commercial potential of university research.

In itself it has contributed to a blurring of any significant line between basic and applied research. Louis Pasteur long ago pronounced that no such line could exist. Nonetheless many scientists have continued to assume that a rough division remains; and, moreover, that whatever profits may be made to flow from applied work, the endeavour in the basic sphere remains to contribute to common understanding of the natural world as a goal above and apart from either politics or commerce. By and large, patent systems have shadowed this understanding. To take again the European example, the systems here are confined to "inventions" as distinct from "discoveries, scientific theories and mathematical methods" (EPC Art 52(2)); and also, really as a rough test of this distinction, by requiring some element of practical utility in what is patentable. (Just what is "capable of industrial application" remains vague; while EPC Art 57 makes it clear that agriculture is a sphere included within "industrial application", it is not clear that it achieves much else. In the US the courts have read into the Patents Act some requirement of practical utility).

There have however been voices arguing that the notion of what is an invention should be pushed even further back into the basic sector of the spectrum. It should be enough, so it is said, to disclose a new piece of scientific information for which there could be potential practical applications. The justification is as for the patent system in general: that protection from the very outset will attract investment in further research and the actual likelihood of beneficial techniques being developed is thereby enhanced. A patent has been compared to a mining licence to explore territory for potential minerals (Kitch 1977; Beier and Straus 1977).

This kind of thinking has found a sudden and dramatic application in the course of HUGO - the remarkable plan to map the entire Human Genome by multi-national collaboration. The project was launched on the basis that findings would be made available to the whole scientific community through data bank networks. In 1992, Craig Venter, an American researcher working in the US under the auspices of the National Institutes of Health, sought to patent several thousand partial sequences of complementary DNA. These were discoveries made in the course of investigating new genes which could act on the central nervous system. However, in many instances, they were not the complete sequence of a gene; nor (it seems) were products isolated or claims made to effective benefits for industry or services such as public health. Patents were being sought merely upon sufficient partial sequencing to characterise a new molecular entity. After a long period of tension, these applications were withdrawn before they reached publication (see e.g. Kiley 1992; HUGO 1993).

The Venter case demonstrates as never before that academic research needs to be undertaken with explicit agreement between researchers, their institutions and outside sponsors or collaborators, about any potential IP. Even an agreement ex post is better than none at all. Certainly the Venter case produced rapid reactions: the MRC made similar patent applications on at least a defensive basis. A number of scientific authorities adopted statements of position, many of them hostile to the Venter initiative (e.g. Institut de France Academie des Sciences 1994).

This often angry response has caught patent systems at a moment when they are still adapting to biotechnology as a phenomenon. While these systems have conceptual tools within them which can be interpreted so as to reach some measure of acceptable balance, there was virtually no experience of how these tools should be applied in the new sphere. But a generally pro-patent approach had been evolving (we shall come back to some of the reasons for it) and this had added impetus to the movement for expanding what can be patented. Much was triggered by the US Supreme Court in *Diamond v Chakrabarty* 65 L Ed 144 (1980). In admitting a US patent on a micro-organism which had been genetically engineered so as to eat oil-slicks, the Court considered "anything under the sun" - apart from human beings themselves - to be patentable (see Armitage 1989). It was a sharp riposte to those who felt real unease over the new directions of research upon living matter and the offering of patent rewards as a technique for encouraging it. In turn, the EPO has been willing to read specific exclusions of plant and animal varieties very narrowly: the result has been to leave open the patenting of genetically engineered animals and plants where the changes are not complex enough to produce a specific new breed or variety (*Lubrizol's Application* [1990] OJ EPO 71).

The withdrawal of the Venter and MRC applications has left us with no legal answer to the question whether they should have led to patents. Ultimately the issue will have to be resolved. One suggestion has been that a distinction should be drawn allowing the patenting of complete gene sequences, but not partial segments. While this may produce a certain clarity, it is likely to appear rather arbitrary. A more satisfactory distinction, and one more in line with the overall purpose of the patent system, lies between genetic developments which are shown to have a practical usefulness, and those which remain purely in the realm of molecular biological description. The distinction between invention and discovery could be read as falling precisely along this divide. If existing patent laws are so read there may be no need for further amendment. But still patent authorities will need to consider what they will accept as sufficient evidence of practical usefulness and there may well be a need to press them to be more stringent than has been the case with, for example, some chemical intermediates.

Reining back the scope of what is patentable by reference to considerations of utility is justified for this reason: so far as can be judged at this stage of development, initiatory work of Venter's type is relatively straightforward, compared with the complex investigations needed to establish uses; yet patents granted on partial sequencing might be of very considerable breadth, requiring a licence from all who put the information to what may prove to be a great variety of uses. That seems a disproportionate preference (Eisenberg 1992; Maebius 1992).

Once one glimpses a commercial Valhalla along a rainbow bridge of intellectual property, the memory is hard to obliterate. Scientists who sense such prospects for their basic investigations will thereafter be less likely to contribute them to public banks of data until a stage is reached at which they can secure their position with a patent or some equivalent protection. This is the essential dilemma. It is being suggested that perhaps some lesser right against unlicensed copying from a Genome data bank would give sufficient protection to induce early deposit of the information in a public source. Some type of copyright has been mentioned, though it is far from clear what limitations are intended to be attached to this right. If it is merely that information should not become available from the source without paying a licence fee for it, then it should be possible to organise this legally through contractual obligations, without the need to create special IP. But a mere charge for access to valuable information is scarcely going to satisfy those who are concerned to turn the information to ultimate commercial advantage. The dilemma, which is by no means a novelty of biotechnology, is not one which can be eradicated by the adjustment of rules about patents or any other kind of intellectual property.

Optimal patenting

Since the early decades of industrialisation, when the patent system first began to flourish and spread, its merits have been contested. When inventors derive so much from their intellectual and social background, does their own contribution to knowledge warrant even a temporary exclusive right in the marketplace? Would not competition provide greater incentive for the introduction of better, more advanced technology? The questions, which have been particularly intense of late from the developing world, ring on. But the system proves to have remarkable resilience. Now more than ever, businesses demand patent protection; its cost is considerable but remains a small fraction of research costs, and even more, of development and marketing expenditure. More realistic questions therefore concern the balance between exclusivity and competition, which is secured through the details of patent law.

The optimal level of patent protection might be put thus: there should be as many patents as there are serious and valuable inventions not previously known. The scope of these rights should be proportionate to the advance in technique involved, and competitors should be able to judge whether alternative products and processes do or do not infringe the rights. These desiderata are difficult to attain. Most patent systems began with essentially a deposit regime: the national patent office granted patents on application and all questions about novelty, inventiveness, adequate disclosure and the like were left to be settled later in court. In industrial countries, this was sooner or later found to let too many patent grants loose on the rest of industry. By way of reaction, pre-grant examination of applications was instituted, and the tendency has been to strengthen this process. In 1977, when the European Patent Convention effected a new deal for numerous states in West Europe, examination was put on a wide basis and had to take place without any deferment so that an industry could know what patents its faced within a set timetable.

It is costly to maintain so scrupulous a system and there are pressures at work to slacken off at various points. Within Europe since 1978, patents may be obtained either by applying to the EPO in Munich for a bundle of national patents or by applying separately to the national patent offices of the countries concerned. These alternative routes necessarily tend to make patent offices applicant-friendly, seeking wherever reasonable to grant patents of the scope sought in the application. It is no longer easy to enjoy a reputation for carping scruple, which in the past belonged to the Dutch and Swiss Patent Offices, though not to them alone. It is now frequently said, particularly by patent professionals in this country, that in some technologies - notably telecommunications and other electronics - the result is an unmanageable swarm of patents, many for very modest alterations of technique, which can nevertheless be asserted by determined owners and prove a costly and distracting business to dispose of by legal challenges to their validity.

Are academics better off with a strict or an indulgent patent system? As sources of invention on a relatively small scale, universities naturally want to get their own patents easily and cheaply. Yet they are, by their size and their distance from the sharp edge of commerce, likely to be worried or put off by the patent claims of others. As far as their own rights are concerned, a patent which has already had a thorough examination forms a good basis for negotiating licences and indeed for attacking infringers. As far as the claims of others are concerned, some certainty about the validity of the rights is likewise a considerable boon. In my judgment, therefore, the interest of the academic community lies in favour of maintaining a careful search and examination system.

There are proposals abroad which would have an undermining effect on this scrupulous approach and therefore deserve to be treated warily. One such is that there should be a second tier of protection, a right which is given for a shorter period than a normal patent and perhaps for technical developments which could not rank as "inventive", but which are not subject to any prior examination. These "petty patents" or "utility models" already exist in nine states of the EU. They differ in detailed rules and their impact varies. They may, for instance, be a useful way of dealing with employee-inventors in systems (such as the German) where the employer has only a short period in which to decide whether to take up rights in the invention or leave it to the employee to exploit. In such countries, most of the applicants for protection are from local industry, rather than from abroad, whether from other EU states or from such frenetically protectionist countries as Japan.

In Britain, the question has been examined quite extensively, since the Chief Scientific Officer to the Cabinet suggested the possibility of a "registered invention right" (Nicholson Report 1983). However, the government refused to include any general second-tier protection for technical ideas as such in the Copyright, Designs and Patents Act 1988 (Department of Trade and Industry 1986). Instead it reformed the law on industrial designs so as to create a new IPR - the so-called unregistered design right, which gives short-term and limited protection to the shape of industrial products and their components against the copying of the particular shape (see MacQueen 1989; Tootal 1990). Now the issue of a general second-tier right seems to be on the agenda again. A plan for an EC right has been propounded, which would give protection in as many Member States as the applicant sought (Max Planck Institute 1994). In this country, some professionals who act for small industry have again raised the question of a UK right and are attempting to assure the British Patent Office that it could be made to pay for itself (Chartered Institute of Patent Agents 1994).

Let me examine the desirability of such a development from the perspective of the academic community. In one sense, the interests of academics align with SMEs. Both can derive advantage from IP as a bargaining card in doing business with large industry, which might otherwise snap its fingers and gobble up the ideas. If therefore there is a form of IP in technology which is relatively cheap to acquire, even if it does not last long, it is tempting to see this as a desirable development. The downside remains, as the government was persuaded before the 1988 Act, that any rights would be of uncertain validity because their novelty and value as an improvement would not have been tested in advance of grant. While academics themselves are not in the business of production, and so do not have to consider directly the extent to which they may infringe the rights of others, any licensee of theirs, large or small, will be in just that position. So what they have to trade may turn out to be a commodity of highly uncertain value. Much more damagingly, third parties (and in particular large industry from round the world) may use these rights to obtain short-term, cheap and wide protection for very modest advances in technology; and their skill in commercial games involving IP is generally of a superior order. For the moment the academic community would do well to examine carefully and sceptically the case for a petty patent or a utility model, however much it is pressed by professional interests. It must be remembered that since 1978, Europe has had applicant friendly system of patent protection, which by its alternative routes provides for the protection of the supra-national and the local invention in ways which at the same time impose controls in the interests of the rest of industry. What most needs improving is the operation of these systems, not the creation of means for side-stepping them.

Self pre-emption

I now reach a point of real and abiding tension between the norms of academic science and those of industry-based patenting. It is the strain which often arises between the scientist's wish to make his work available to his peers and the demand of the protectors that this should not happen until all relevant patent applications have been made, and that indeed there should be a legal obligation of confidence in the information until that point.

It is an ironic conflict, since the patent system also seeks to make inventions public when otherwise they might be kept secret. To Anglicise the matter: as "consideration" for the grant, the patentee must describe his invention in the patent specification to an extent that will allow a person skilled in the art to understand its characteristics. The problem is accordingly a disparity of timing (Eisenberg 1987).

Let me not fall into the lawyer's happy assumption that his coordinates of action have a natural superiority. The desire of academic scientists to make their research results available with despatch is something much more complex than an abstract devotion to an outmoded public good. Basic science depends for its validity and reliability on the speedy, widespread dissemination of novel research results, so as to expose them immediately to critical analysis and hoped-for acceptance. This is the only real way of purging them of errors and misconceptions. For all the personal rivalries between academic scientists, and occasional secretiveness in the race for priority, they insist on the importance of publishing new data and theories as soon as they can be presented as sound and convincing. Indeed, this openness is a necessary condition for any system of personal recognition for scientific excellence. Academic scientists are thus subject to a highly competitive system of quality control, which provides the framework for innumerable well-established procedures, from the peer review of papers and grant applications, and the obligation to cite earlier work, to the award of Nobel Prizes.

Why then does the patent system insist that application must come before making the invention public, even when this is done by the very person who is seeking protection? Patents give a right that is good against the world including others who independently reach the same invention; they are not merely rights against those who copy. Truly successful inventions are ideas which a whole industry is likely to want to copy, and the power of an exclusive right in such circumstances can be realised only when the patent extends to all the various ways in which the invention might be implemented in products or processes. Potentially, then, it is an economically powerful weapon and is made available only under limited conditions. In most systems the patent goes to the first among competing inventors who applies for it (the Americans however conduct intricate investigations, where necessary, into the question who was the first to invent). That is a considerable incentive to get the invention out into the open as soon as possible. But in addition all systems demand that the information be novel, just as most now add that it must also be inventive over the existing state of the art, measured at a priority date which is fixed in relation to application. The effect of this is that no one may have a patent in information which has been made sufficiently public; and in particular an inventor may not publish his ideas, wait for their potential to be visible in the market-place and then seek his period of exclusivity.

The current European principles were drafted in the 1970s, at a time when intellectual property rights were under considerable suspicion from various quarters, not least from the proponents of positive, legally-enforced competition in the EC. The patent laws, for which government officials from patent offices were largely responsible, opted for substantive rules and procedures, which were to be efficient, swift and severe. Accordingly they introduced a test of so-called absolute novelty on the lines which I have already sketched, and they allowed the applicants for patents virtually no leeway in the matter of earlier publication or public use: such conduct would produce "self pre-emption".

It is not necessary to be so tough. The former British law had a number of exceptions allowing inventors to sanction the exhibition of their inventions in certain ways and to read papers about them at learned societies and still within six months to apply for patents (Patents Act 1949 ss 50, 51). The US Patents Act has a general "grace period" discounting publications anywhere and public use of an invention in the US in relation to any patent application bearing a priority date within the ensuing twelve months. In the present state of play, academics everywhere gain twelve months' grace in relation to US patenting while in Europe they are under a strict time discipline. Since everyone tends to think primarily in terms of their own local rules, this differential can prove to be more of a trap to American inventors than to their European counterparts.

There is certainly a case for introducing a single standard around the world and it has been hoped that agreement on this issue among others could be reached in the project of the World Intellectual Property Organisation for a Patent Law Harmonisation Treaty. The compromise which had been emerging in the negotiations for that instrument sought the introduction of an agreed grace period in return for adoption in the US of a first-to-file, rather than a first-to-invent system. But the US is proving reluctant to pursue these negotiations and it looks as though there can be no international resolution of the basic ground rule in the near future.

At present a grace period is a typically American phenomenon and it will not be adopted elsewhere save as part of a larger project for harmonisation. Other countries hesitate to introduce one because inevitably it makes for complications and expense. Advisors considering whether a technical idea can be adopted must look not only at the patents granted and applied for in the territory in question but must search the literature for any appearance of the concept which within twelve months may give rise to an application. This suits carefully organised corporate entities which can insist that their research staff keep everything under wraps at least until the patent department or outside agent gives the all clear.

The environment in which academic work is conducted is different. Researchers do not readily extract an oath of secrecy from all the participants at a staff seminar; if they were to do so, they would, in the hard world of invention exploitation, need unrockable evidence that they got the promise from everyone - latecomers, special visitors, those who have dropped in for a bit of competitive snooping. As a result the eager and inexperienced on occasion let out secrets which may jeopardise subsequent patenting, while leading figures who have their eye on the patent stakes find themselves obliged to offer their Royal Society audiences only anticipatory glimpses, since they must discreetly veil what might otherwise be a compromising revelation.

These prospects are bothersome but their inevitability in the current scheme of things has to be faced. The introduction or not of a grace period will turn, as has been indicated, on the grand politics of international patent negotiations. Academic interests are not likely to have much influence on their outcome, since in all countries the contribution of academic research to the volume of patented invention remains small. In consequence, the academic community must look after its own interests as best it can. Since it is now bent on extracting commercial value from research where that is possible, there are two obvious steps for it to take. One is to improve the extent of knowledge of the patent system and its processes of operation among the scientific community. There may then be a growing realisation that while the system may have its awkwardnesses, it is not so wholly antagonistic to academic values as to deserve only contempt. The other is for those who administer the acquisition of rights in or for universities to sharpen their procedures. It should be possible to get patenting business promptly in hand, while ensuring that only preliminary and confidential steps are taken to arrange the publication of material before patent applications are made. In this there needs to be greater readiness among some scientific publishers and editors to accept material and put it to assessors under conditions of secrecy. If this is done, the patenting position will not be jeopardised.

Ethical issues

Finally I want to avert briefly to the ethical isssues in patenting certain kinds of technological novelties. Science and the technologies which flow from it, more than ever before, offer opportunities for altering and improving health, nourishment, experience, enjoyment; and at the same time, intentionally or unintentionally, for producing personal, social and environmental evils on horrific scales. Patent systems are designed by states specifically to foster technical advances with practical effects, to spread knowledge of them, and to encourage the investment which will convert them into commercial successes; these systems can scarcely stand aside from the moral dilemmas which modern science hurls at us so unceasingly. We may accept that patent systems embody their own moral imperative: the intellectual achievement of making and publishing an invention deserves to be recognised in the grant of a limited proprietary right. But invention can scarcely rank as an automatic good, requiring no balancing against other considerations. The issue is by no means confined to the academic laboratory. But since many of the current questions arise in the context of biotechnology, where academic institutions are so much at the forefront of developments, it seems apposite at least to avert to the problem in the present framework.

There are certainly voices, particularly from within patent offices and patent professions, which urge that the granting of rights should be a matter purely of technical assessment. They claim that questions whether an invention is too harmful to be allowed should be determined by authorities with a power of prevention (such as the health and safety inspectors who stepped in recently to arrest cancer virus work at Birmingham University), not within a system which is concerned only with the reward of commercial exclusivity. They point out that patent office examiners have no special expertise in moral assessment.

However, under the EPC, patents are not to be granted for inventions, the publication or exploitation of which is contrary to *ordre public* or morality (EPC, Art 53(a), which adds the proviso that it is not enough to offend this provision that 'the invention is prohibited by law or regulation in some or all of the Convention states - see also Patents Act 1977 s 1(3)). Patent authorities in Europe are accordingly drawn, at least in some measure, beyond the purely technical arena. It was that plucky but doomed little figure, the Oncomouse, invented at Harvard but commercially owned, who has given the matter such recent prominence (see Beyleveld and Brownsword 1993 and Hudson 1992).

Recognising that the need to balance conflicting concerns was unavoidable in the circumstances, the EPO has so far allowed the patent application to proceed to grant, but now has to deal with a battery of objections from third parties under the post-grant opposition procedure. It has chosen so far to apply a felicific calculus in which the ultimate benefits to humankind from cancer research were found to outweigh the measure of suffering inflicted on the genetically manipulated animals..

The underlying distaste of patent professionals for this arena of debate, however, has been expressed in the course of a rather less sentimental, but equally committed, opposition before the EPO (*Greenpeace UK v Plant Genetic Systems* (1993) 24 IIC 618). Greenpeace objected, mainly on the morality ground, to the patenting of crops and their genetic materials which possess a foreign gene encoding resistance to glutamine synthetase inhibitors; in other words, of plants genetically engineered to survive certain weedkillers, when all around are succumbing. Greenpeace's principal arguments went to the potential dangers inherent in releasing such plant material in the environment. The organisation raised a general objection to ecological disturbance by genetic manipulation; but specifically argued against a practice which would release into the natural world plants with a resistance to weedkillers.

The Opposition Division has rejected these objections by a variety of arguments, the worst of which purvey a sense of acute discomfort with the whole business. For instance, it is said in the Decision, ignoring the whole incentive purpose of patenting, that an invention, even if refused a patent, is likely to be exploited anyway. And at one stage, the Division pronounces that any willingness to enter on moral investigations would lead to it having to deal with "controversial and 'fashionable' inventions" under oppositions raised by "possibly specialist groups", while "less visible but possibly objectively equally offensive inventions would go through unopposed" (Opinion, paras 3.4, 3.9, 3.10). Tightly packed adverbs may indicate deep embarrassment but they do little to cure it. They also read like code for refusing any truck with the dotty ideas of noisy weirdos. I suspect, however, that the message was encrypted just because the opponents were felt to be raising issues of some real concern, which the Tribunal might have been inclined to take more seriously if only the rest of the world would.

The Decision proceeded to discuss the unquestionable difficulty in any dispute over moral or social values: how to determine the range of views and how to strike a balance between them. In addition to considerable scientific evidence, Greenpeace provided a survey, purporting to show (as one must say of any survey) that 80 per cent of Swedish farmers were against the release of weed-killer resistant plants into the environment. Even if a true test of opinion, this said nothing about the opinion of farmers elsewhere in the EPO net of countries, nor about the opinion of non-farmers anywhere.

Nonetheless, it cannot be right to hold out the incentive of a patent (which many will read as an imprimatur) for things and activities with obviously harmful or improper primary uses, such as letter bombs, instruments of torture, and instruments for inhaling dangerous substances. If this is so, then some Tribunal has to decide what must be excluded. Legislation goes some way at present, but there could never be a complete list in advance. Given that not granting a patent has no prohibitory effect, and given also that in many cases the invention will have benign as well as malign applications, it is sensible to exclude inventions only in cases where the arguments for doing so are plainly the stronger. But to have a high presumption of validity on these issues is one thing; to deny that each case should be dealt with on its merits is quite another and is an attempt to root the issue out of patent law altogether. That should not happen.

The duty to make the assessment should remain, and it should continue to be placed on the shoulders of those who take the decision on the admissibility of applications and patents in other respects. There is no indication that the moral issues will become so constant and intractable that a separate decision-making body is called for. The emphasis that there has been on the inabilities of examiners in patent offices ignores the fact that they are but the first line in a more elaborate framework of judicial authority. In the EPO, for instance, appeal lies to Appeal Boards on which legally trained judges also sit (and lawyers are confident in deciding most things). Once national patents are granted, their validity may be attacked not only by opposition in the EPO but also in each national jurisdiction. This at least allows for the patent to be invalidated in any country where a particular objection can be sustained - Sweden, for instance, if there really is a considerable objection there to the production of crops resistant to weedkillers.

Conclusion

I began with the managerial sea-change by which universities and similar academic bodies are seeking to capitalise upon the commercial consequences of their research output. This shift is a re-orientation, but it is as yet far from being a revolution. The road from inventive perception to royalty-returning products or processes is a hard and risky one. Even US campuses, such as MIT and Stanford, which have a substantial history of this sort of work, only show a return of under 5 per cent of total research budget; in those British universities which have moved farthest in this direction, the equivalent figure would be between 1-2%. It is not possible to expect TTUs to be financially self-sufficient at an early stage, let alone plan that a significant part of necessary and desirable research expenditure should come by way of commercial return. Equally, academic research should not be evaluated by reference either to the granting of patents or the returns upon them, rather than on the inherent merits of the work done.

My concern today has been to examine a number of points in the operation of patent systems which in this new atmosphere are contributing to a sense of unease in the academic community. My discussion of them has I hope been informed by a sense of how experimental the re-orientation still is. For the moment it deserves a fair wind, but it must not itself whip up storms of hostility and protest where this can be avoided. That applies as much to basic legal rules and their administration by courts and patent offices as it does to R&D managers within and without universities and research institutes. We will begin to approach a level of acceptability only if we face problems realistically. This means a widespread diffusion of knowledge about what is going on. There has to be a lot of short-term instruction among scientists, and some longer-term training of research managers and exploiters, in the nature of intellectual property and its place in the complex process of turning scientific knowledge to industrial account. Already many more people are aware of the chances and the hazards than even five years ago. It has become a most interesting time.

This is a revised version of the Miller Lecture, delivered in the Faculty of Law, University of Edinburgh on February 14, 1994. During the time of its preparation, I have chaired a working party of the National Academies Policy Advisory Group (NAPAG) on Intellectual Property and the Academic Community, on which subject NAPAG is to present a Report in the autumn of 1994. The views expressed in this lecture are entirely my own, but I gratefully acknowledge the shape that they have taken through the discussions on that Working Party and from the information collected during its deliberations.

Legal Economics

Antony W Dnes

Synopsis

This paper serves as an introduction to the economic analysis of law, highlighting in particular the economics of crime with special reference to murder and theft, the property-based wrong of nuisance (which has been one of the bases for the protection of privacy under existing law), and breach of contract. The contribution which economic analysis of law can make to the study of economics generally is highlighted.

✳✳✳✳

There has been a considerable recent growth of interest on this side of the Atlantic in combining the study of law and economics into a specialist sub-discipline, which is best referred to as 'legal economics'. This follows after a long-standing development of the subject in the USA. The link between economic analysis and legal principles and practice has long been recognized by writers on regulatory topics, particularly in the case of competition policy. The newer work on legal economics goes much further and applies economic analysis to legal instruments, questions and procedures.

In some respects, integrating economic analysis with legal studies is not new. Certainly, in the eighteenth and nineteenth centuries it was more common for political economists to work on much more institutionally focused questions than has been the case in the recent past. Thus, in the *Wealth of Nations*, Adam Smith saw primogeniture and the English Poor Laws as inhibiting the economic development of society in its move from mercantilism towards industrialism. Primogeniture caused land to be transferred in large parcels, which in practice meant some of it often remained unused. The Poor Laws, much like public housing in our time, made labour mobility difficult as the labourer was restricted from moving to another parish - a policy intended to stop the poor of one parish becoming a burden on landowners in another. The study of legal economics is a two-way process: there are questions about the economic efficiency of the law and about the necessity of law to economic efficiency.

In the recent past, many economists moved away from such a focus on the economic questions of the day. The university-based subject became rather over-concerned with formal and somewhat arid economic modelling (I exempt the think tanks from this criticism). Legal economics counteracts such a trend because it necessarily focuses on the economic implications of real-world legal instruments, questions and procedures. It is not alone in maintaining such an institutional orientation. Other areas, like public choice (the economics of politics) and the economics of organization, also do the same thing. I share the critical optimism of Sam Peltzman (1991), who believes that the tide has turned. High theory has over-reached itself and the days of arid formalism are probably coming to a close.

My comments should not be misinterpreted as a criticism of the use of mathematics and statistics in economic analysis. Clearly these techniques can be useful. Researchers in legal economics use modern techniques such as game theory to make predictions about real-world situations, and apply statistical methods such as time-series analysis to test the predictions. It is all a question of purpose: in legal economics the focus is very definitely on the application of relevant techniques to institutional questions.

Since economics studies rational behaviour, defined as the pursuit of consistent ends by efficient means (Cooter and Ulen 1988), there is no difficulty in applying it to the law. Ends and means are clearly involved in setting and administering the law. A few simple examples of legal cases and issues will clarify what is meant by this application. I draw them from the classic areas of law to show that economic analysis can be fruitfully applied to some common questions.

The economics of crime

I start with an example from criminal law as there is undoubtedly a great concern world-wide with the breakdown of law and order.

Some countries in the Far East impose death sentences on those convicted of smuggling hard drugs. Economic analysis shows why this might make sense. These countries are relatively poor and probably cannot afford to devote large amounts of money to detecting smugglers. If criminals are rational, they will respond to increases in the expected value of punishment by reducing their criminal activity. This response will follow even if criminals are often driven by irrational factors, as long as they react rationally at the margin of their activities (Buchanan and Hartley 1992).

The expected value of punishment equals the probability of conviction multiplied by the sentence for the crime. If a country cannot afford to increase the conviction rate, it can obtain the same effect in reducing smuggling by adopting severe sentences. The economist Gary Becker (1968) has conjectured that this trade-off explains the existence of severe punishments for non-capital crimes in earlier times in what are now more advanced societies.

A contemporary practical application of the type of reasoning involved in comparing deterrence through severity with that from probability of conviction is easy to make. Most modern societies are concerned about increasing levels of both violent and property crime. How should this be tackled? If the cost of increasing the severity of prison sentences is compared with that for increasing detection and conviction of criminals, it turns out to be much cheaper to obtain a target reduction in crime by increasing the length of sentences (Pyle 1989). The economic analysis here is useful. It suggests that the common response of many governments around the world to rising crime - to increase expenditure on police - may not be the most cost effective. Interestingly, it seems we have not moved that far from the predicament facing less developed countries: albeit that their severity is more severe!

On a more philosophical note, it is interesting to note that all societies have strong laws or prohibitions against theft. This is because property crime is always wasteful and economic efficiency requires that it be deterred. The thief devotes resources to his activity that might go towards making new products, and he may value his gains less highly than does his victim. The victim must spend money defending himself. Theft is massively wasteful. Societies in which social codes strongly reinforce law abiding behaviour enjoy the advantage of avoiding such waste. Once property rights have been defined, their protection is absolutely crucial to the prosperity of society.

Curiously, the same taboo does not exist through all societies concerning murder. For example, Eskimo societies were known to condone the murder of ungenerous rich people. Nevertheless, the reason for this was almost certainly related to political economy. In such a society, traditions such as 'potlatch' (the periodic giving away of one's wealth) were probably a means for preventing the emergence of despotic government. An individual who grew wealthy could have amassed retainers and ruled the others. The murders, apart from being an emergency measure in this respect, reinforced the incentive to be generous (Posner 1980). However, potlatch was probably a reason why these societies never progressed beyond the nomadic, hunter-gatherer stage, as the incentive to accumulate was clearly absent. Growth may have been traded for political freedom.

The economics of nuisance

My second substantial example comes from the legal treatment of nuisance, which is a 'tort' - or private wrongdoing - in common law countries like the UK and USA, or, in Scotland, a 'delict'. In the famous case of *Sturges v Bridgman* (1879) 11 Ch D 852, a confectioner set up shop next to a physician, whom he disturbed with the vibration and noise from equipment. The doctor (Sturges) won the right to stop the noise. What are the economic implications of this?

Economists regard *Sturges* as a case of 'externality' - i.e. there are spillover effects caused by conflicting property rights. Ronald Coase (now a Nobel prize winner) analysed *Sturges* extensively in his 1960 article 'The Problem of Social Cost'. A general point that Coase emphasised was the inherently reciprocal nature of externalities: the confectioner affects the doctor but the latter has to be in the way for harm to arise. Both parties are exercising legitimate private property rights, which conflict. Coase reached the surprising conclusion that it does not matter in these cases whether the person causing the nuisance (Bridgman) has the right to continue or whether the victim has the right to stop him, as long as they can bargain at reasonably low cost. The costs of bargaining must not exceed the benefits the bargainer hopes to receive.

According to this version of the 'Coase theorem', if the costs of moving the confectioner exceed the costs of moving the doctor, the confectioner can bribe him to move. To help see this, assume the profits of each party exceed the other one's moving costs and are invariant with location. However, the doctor's profits are reduced by more than his moving costs if he stays put, and the confectioner has the highest moving costs. Moving the doctor is the efficient result, which the confectioner's bribe would achieve. The confectioner would rather pay the doctor to move as it is cheaper for him. The doctor would rather move with his costs fully paid, as he then continues to make the same profit.

If on the other hand the confectioner had won the right to continue his nuisance (which he did not) the doctor could have tried to bribe him to stop, and would have been willing to pay up to his own removal costs. The doctor's bribe will not be enough and he will have to move. Again this is the efficient result: the lower-cost mover does the moving and combined profits are as high as they can be.

In this version of the Coase theorem, the assignment of rights (an injunction in *Sturges*) has no efficiency implications although it does have a *distributional* impact. The doctor is worse off without the injunction as he pays his own costs.

Coase went on to show that where bargaining is ruled out by high costs of negotiation, the courts needed to make an informed economic comparison because their ruling will have an *efficiency* impact. They should check whether the profits of the confectioner *plus* those of the doctor are highest after subtracting the removal costs of the doctor. If this is so then the confectioner should have the right to continue. If not, then the doctor should have an injunction so that the confectioner moves. To achieve efficiency it is also necessary that compensation be paid to the doctor if the nuisance prevails, so as to give the confectioner an incentive to adopt noise-reducing technology if this were more cheaply available.

One observation on the operation of the law in nuisance cases like *Sturges* is that it tends to award an injunction rather than award compensatory damages wherever the number of parties is small. This would seem to be efficient, since this is when bargaining costs are likely to be low. If such rules become well known to holders of property rights they may avoid taking their disputes to court, preferring to settle at an earlier stage and avoid the costs of litigation. The law can then be seen as operating along the lines of 'rule' as opposed to 'act' utilitarianism: i.e. the law selects a rule that encourages efficient behaviour rather than trying to calculate who should move in each case. Utilitarianism is not a precise analogy if Posner (1992) is correct in arguing that the purpose of law is wealth maximization (comparison of monetary gains and losses) rather than utility maximization (differentially weighting the gains and losses to different people).

It is surprising how often Coase's insight over finding the least-cost way to resolve conflicting rights is overlooked. Governments often intervene in the economy ostensibly in an effort to control nuisances flowing from conflicting rights. For example, environmental controls are often bureaucratically determined and applied, which then raise industrial costs. However, in recent years there have been some attempts to see whether alternatives like marketable pollution permits could work, which is equivalent to allowing bargaining around an injunction favouring a clean environment. Schemes of marketable permits have been introduced in Australia, New Zealand and the USA, for example. These experiments are encouraging and show that market-based systems of pollution control are feasible.

There is no guarantee that statutorily imposed rules are the right ones from the point of view of voters and taxpayers. Legislative processes can frequently become captured by special outside interest groups, or may reflect the interests of politicians themselves. It is more than likely, for example, that taxation of petroleum is aimed more at funding large government than at controlling the environment. Regulation of industries often protects incumbent firms from entry, in which case policy has become 'captured' (Stigler 1971) as may well have been the case with US airline regulation, for example. On balance over the long run of history, the impartial common-law system should do better at balancing competing claims because it is probably more difficult to capture an independent judiciary than an elected body. It should be noted, however, that some commentators on the common law at the present time would not see efficiency. There is a strong tendency to talk of justice in the 'individual case', which usually means ex post analysis with harmful effects for those making decisions on the basis of apparently settled precedents. Nevertheless, the common law has rights of appeal to a series of judges that should mitigate such tendencies compared with statute.

The economics of breach of contract

My final example is drawn from the study of contract. Economic efficiency is based on voluntary trading, which is supported by a law of contract that enforces terms of trade and may plug gaps in agreements that would otherwise be too costly to cover. Contract law enables resources to be transferred to their most valuable uses, as people come to know what promises are enforceable and how enforcement may occur. The law also rules out contracts based on fraud, duress or misunderstanding.

Suppose a company does not wish to complete a service it has promised to undertake. Should it be forced to perform? Both economics and law suggest the answer is 'no', except in special cases. The reason is simple. It is not the business of the law to force people to carry out tasks for which the economic justification may have disappeared, but only to ensure they compensate for their non-performance. There is such a thing as efficient breach of contract, when the breacher is able to compensate the 'victim' for non-performance. The special cases arise when unique goods or services are involved, and the courts will invoke the (equitable) remedy of specific performance; the promisor is required to carry out his promise because in these cases the value to the promisee is hard to determine owing to uniqueness, and assessment of compensation is costly.

In a famous case, *Tsakiroglou & Co Ltd v Noblee Thorl GmbH* [1962] AC 93, a company in the Sudan undertook to sell peanuts to a German firm on standard terms - in particular, at a price including insurance and freight. The Suez war erupted in 1956 and the company claimed delivery was impossible. The buyer claimed delivery was just more expensive (around the Cape) and won. The case is particularly useful as an illustration of the insurance function of contracts.

The courts concentrated upon the issue of whether performance was physically possible. The economic issue is not this, but rather whether the risk was assigned and if not then who should bear it. The economist sees a contract as an attempt to increase efficiency by allocating future contingencies between the parties. By dealing with contingencies and allocating risks, contracts perform an insurance function (Posner 1992: 126). In *Tsakiroglou*, it seems the seller was in the best position - *at the time the contract was written* - to cover the contingency of blockage of the canal. It is also relevant that the price included insurance and freight, suggesting these things were the responsibility of the seller. The courts probably got this one right for the wrong (stated) reasons.

The general economic point here is that contracts should assign risks to those best able to bear them. This is a useful principle for courts when they are asked to enforce a contract. If businesses discerned such a general tendency in the courts, they could save themselves the costs of covering these details in contracts, unless they wished explicitly to do something else - which the courts would have to respect. The courts perform a role in lowering transactions costs in business. Again, if firms can see how the courts will rule, they will probably settle disputes privately.

Concluding comments

The examples I have just considered show how economists have made contributions to some classic legal areas. Of course, some economists (and others) always analysed regulatory issues and their work was an early kind of legal economics mainly concerned with antitrust and the regulation of natural monopoly. A recent contribution of economists to shaping the law can be seen in US antitrust, where economic argument led in the 1980s to a more accommodating view of vertical contractual relations between firms. In recent years, there have been extensions into many more areas such as patent law and intellectual property, labour law, family law, and sexual regulation.

The economist's main role in much of this new, institutionally focused work is to compare carefully the costs and benefits of proposals in realistic settings. This contrasts with much recent pure economic theory that has made 'nirvana' comparisons between impossible ideal states, characterised unrealistically by an absence of costs for government intervention (Demsetz 1969). Of course, costless government can solve anything. It is real ones that cause problems or fail to solve them.

I am cautiously optimistic, that the result of the development of legal economics, along with that of other institutionally focused areas like public choice and the economics of organisation, is to return us to a more useful type of economic analysis. This is essentially an applied study of use to the general public. We might usefully follow the example of Adam Smith: as Viner (1927) points out, whenever Smith was faced with a conflict between theory and facts in the *Wealth of Nations*, to his credit, he went with the facts.

Notes

Martin A Hogg, **The Very Private Life of the Right to Privacy**

1. What is meant here is not that the legal rules relating to confidentiality and privacy are identical, for the law of confidence has many particular restrictions, but that the concepts of 'private' and 'confidential' have similar meanings in an abstract, semantic sense, and that where information is concerned, the law protecting 'confidential' information can be seen as relevant to a discussion of the law protecting 'private' information.
2. In other words, if the person who is the originator of the information views it in a confidential way, then this strengthens the case for an obligation of confidence attaching to it; and the contrary also applies. Hence, information about one's sex life might usually be subject to the obligation of confidence, but this could be negated if a person has no care as to whether such a subject is discussed by others. Consider, though, *Woodwards v Hutchins* [1977] 1 WLR 760, which suggests that it will be hard to complain that one is taking a restrictive attitude towards a certain piece of information, when this has not been the case previously with regard to all other similar types of information.
3. Are any other factors relevant? The Scottish Law Commission (1984: para 4.16) suggested that three relevant factors might be (i) the nature of the information; (ii) the relationship between the recipient and the person from whom the information is received; and (iii) the manner and circumstances in which the information was received.
4. Though use by an individual of public places with some degree of privacy (such as public conveniences, or changing cubicles in sports facilities) might raise privacy aspects also.
5. Personal data is data, that is, information recorded in a form in which it can be processed by equipment operating automatically in response to instructions given for that purpose, consisting of information which relates to a living individual who can be identified from that information.

W R Cornish, **Scientific Research and Intellectual Property**

1.   The position in regard to patents is by no means the same when it comes to copyright (a) because there is no statutory obligation on an employer who acquires an employee's copyright to pay adequate remuneration for it, whereas such an obligation exists in relation to patents (see Patents Act 1977, ss 40-43); and (b) because copyright determines the right to publish or not publish and so is closely bound up with an essential academic freedom.

2.   The EPO route has proved a signal success, most significant patentees preferring this route on grounds of simplicity and cost-saving. Within the frame of 17 countries now participating in the EPC, the EU states have their own project for a Community Patent, which has existed in Convention form since 1975 but is beset by issues concerning translations of specifications and other difficulties. So it remains a paper proposal.

3.   One starting point was the Strasbourg Convention on the Unification of Certain Points of Substantive Law on Patents for Invention, 1963 (Council of Europe).

4.   For the present, it is thought by governments to be impossible to procure any amendment of the EPC. Within the EU, it is possible to engage in the lateral strategy of requiring amendments to *national* patent law by the enactment of Directives. It is this course which is being pursued in the proposed Directive on the Legal Protection of Biotechnological Inventions (4148/93, COM(92)589).

5.   It may be that, at least in Europe, the patenting of any aspect of the human genome, even when detached from the body, will be rendered unpatentable. An amendment to the proposed EU Directive on the Legal Protection of Biotechnological Inventions is currently before the European Parliament. This seems too indiscriminate a condemnation of biotechnological research activity in the medical sphere to pass into actual legislation, but it is likely to be the subject of intense debate.

6.   There are now 17 states, within and beyond the EU, which participate in the EPC.

7.   The Netherlands is poised to become the tenth, leaving only the UK and Luxembourg without such a system.

8.   The European Commission is considering the question whether there should be action at EU level, either by way of Regulation or by a harmonisation directive. It proposes to produce a Green Paper which canvasses the arguments; but it will not press the case for intervention to the extent of including a draft measure.

9.   The potential for such behaviour is much increased if the system follows the modern trend of allowing second tier protection for substances and processes, as well as the form of mechanical devices (which was the older approach comprehended in the description, "utility model"); and of allowing claims to all variants of the protected concept which satisfy a substantive test which is lower than the obviousness test of patent law. These broad ideas are incorporated, for instance, in the proposal for an EU Utility Model.

10. Under some systems, including that in Britain before the 1977 Act, this
was policed by making prior secret use, as well as prior publication and
prior public use, a ground of invalidity. In the European concordat, only
prior publication and use that amounts to a publication count as objections: see EPC, Arts 52, 54, 56.

11. The Draft Directive on the Legal Protection of Biotechnological Inventions accepts that the present approach contained in the EPC will
continue. (The Council has now reached a common position on the
Directive, but the confirmatory proceedings in the European Parliament
threaten to destroy that harmony.) It seeks to add a measure of specificity
in the biotechnological area. This approach is largely accepted by the
House of Lords (1994).

12. The Draft Directive on Biotechnological Inventions now seeks, so far as
possible, to define exclusions by specific rules: thus it would eliminate
patents for the human body or its parts per se (i.e. when not separated
from the body), and processes for modifying the genetic identity of
animals which are likely to inflict suffering or physical handicaps upon
them without any benefit to man or animal. To this is added a further
category: processes for modifying the genetic identity of the human body
for a non-therapeutic purpose which is contrary to the dignity of man.
The opacity of this proposition led the House of Lords (1994: para 51) to
recommend its deletion; but something of the kind must be said once the
path is chosen. Whether the Directive is going to survive in this or any
other form is currently an open question.

Bibliography

Armitage, E., (1989). The emerging US patent law for the protection of biotechnology research results. *European Intellectual Property Review*, **11**, 47.

Becker, G., (1968). Crime and punishment: an economic approach. *Journal of Political Economy*, **69**, 169-217.

Beier, F-K., and Straus, J., (1977). The patent system and the information function yesterday and today. *International Review of Industrial Property and Copyright*, **8**, 387.

Bell, G. J., (1899). *Principles of the law of Scotland.* 10th ed. Edinburgh.

Bell, G. J., (1871). *Commentaries on the law of Scotland and the principles of mercantile jurisprudence.* 7th ed. Edinburgh.

Beyleveld, R., and Brownsword, R., (1993). *Mice, morality and patents.* London: Common Law Institute of Intellectual Property.

Bos, M., (1991). *The diffusion of heart and liver transplantation across Europe.* London: King's Fund Centre.

Brams, M., (1977). Transplantable human organs: should their sale be authorized by state statutes? *American Journal of Law and Medicine*, **3**, 183.

Buchanan, C., and Hartley, P. R., (1992). *Criminal choice: the economic theory of crime and its implications for crime control.* CIS Policy Monograph 24.

Cabinet Office (1992). *Intellectual property and the public sector research base.* London: HMSO

Cabinet Office (1993). *Realising our potential.* Cm 2250. London: HMSO.

Calcutt Report (1990). *Privacy and related matters.* Cm 1102. London: HMSO.

Calcutt Report (1993). *Review of press self-regulation.* Cm 2135. London: HMSO.

Chadwick, R. F., (1989). The market for bodily parts: Kant and duties to oneself. *Journal of Applied Philosophy*, **6**, 129.

Chartered Institute of Patent Agents (1994). *Second tier protection.* London.

Coase, R., (1960). The problem of social cost. *Journal of Law and Economics*, **3**, 1-44.

Cooter, T., and Ulen, T., (1988). *Law and economics.* New York: Harper Collins.

Cornish, W. R., (1992). Rights in university innovations. *European Intellectual Property Review*, 14, 13.

Demsetz, H., (1969). Information and efficiency: another viewpoint. *Journal of Law and Economics*, **12**, 1-22.

Department of Trade and Industry (1986). *Intellectual property and innovation.* Cmnd 9445. London: HMSO.

Devlin, P., (1965). *The enforcement of morals.* London : Oxford University Press.

Eisenberg, R. S., (1987). Proprietary rights and the norms of science in biotechnology research. *Yale Law Journal*, **97**, 177.

Eisenberg, R. S., (1992). Genes, patents and product development. *Science*, **257**, 903.

Erskine, J., (1871). *An institute of the law of Scotland.* 8th ed. Edinburgh.

Feinberg, J., (1988). *The moral limits of the criminal law*. 4 vols. New York: Oxford University Press.
Gavison, R., (1980). Privacy and the limits of the law. *Yale Law Journal*, **89**, 421.
George, R. P., (1993). *Making men moral*. Oxford: Clarendon Press.
Gurry, F., (1984). *Breach of confidence*. Oxford: Clarendon Press.
Harris, J., (1992). *Wonderwoman and superman*. Oxford: Oxford University Press.
Hart, H. L. A., (1963). *Law, liberty and morality*. Oxford: Oxford University Press.
Haworth, L., (1986). *Autonomy*. New Haven and London: Yale University Press.
Hill, T. E., (1991). *Autonomy and self respect*. Cambridge: Cambridge University Press.
Hogg, M. A., (1992). Privacy: a valuable and protected interest in Scots law. *Scots Law Times*, News, 349.
House of Lords (1994). *Patent protection for biotechnological inventions*. Select Committee on the European Communities, HL Paper 28.
HUGO (1993). *Intellectual property in genome mapping programmes*. Workshop Report, 20-22 November.
Husack, D. N., (1992). *Drugs and rights*. Cambridge: Cambridge University Press.
Institut de France Académie des Sciences (1994). *The patentability of the genome*. Paris.
Joubert, W. A., (1976-). *The law of South Africa*. 30 vols. Durban: Butterworths.
Kiley, T. D., (1992). Patents on random complementary DNA fragments. *Science*, **257**, 915.
Kitch, E. W., (1977). The nature and function of the patent system. *Journal of Law and Economics*, **20**, 265.
Kleinig, J., (1991). *Valuing life*. Princeton: Princeton University Press.
Lord Chancellor's Department and Scottish Office (1993). *Consultation paper on infringement of privacy*. London: Central Office of Information.
MacQueen, H. L., (1989). *Copyright, competition and industrial design*. Aberdeen: Aberdeen University Press for The David Hume Institute.
MacQueen, H. L., (1993). Breach of confidence. In *The laws of Scotland: Stair memorial encyclopedia*, **18**, paras 1451-1500. London and Edinburgh: Butterworths.
Maebius, S.B., (1992). Novel DNA sequences and the utility requirement: the human genome initiative. *Journal of the Patent Office Society*, **74**, 651.
Mason, J. K., and McCall Smith, R. A., (1994). *Law and medical ethics*. 4th ed. London: Butterworths.
May, W., (1972). Attitudes toward the newly dead. *Hastings Center Studies*, **1**, 3.
Max Planck Institute for foreign and international Patent, Copyright and Competition Law. Proposal for a European Utility Model (1994).
Munzer, S. R., (1994). An uneasy case against property rights in body parts. *Social Philosophy and Policy*, **2**, 259.
National Heritage Select Committee (1993). *Privacy and media intrusion*. London: HMSO.
Nicholson Report (1983). *Intellectual property and innovation*. Cmnd 9117. London: HMSO.
Peltzman, S., (1991). The handbook of industrial organisation: a review article. *Journal of Political Economy*, **91**, 201-217.
Perry, C., (1980). Human organs and the open market. *Ethics*, **91**, 63.
Posner, R., (1980). A theory of primitive society with special reference to the law. *Journal of Law and Economics*, **23**, 1-53.
Posner, R., (1992). *Economic analysis of law*. 4th ed. Boston: Little Brown & Co.
Pyle, D., (1989). The economics of crime in Britain. *Economic Affairs*, **9**, 6-9.
Scottish Law Commission (1977). *Confidential information*. Consultative Memorandum no 40. Edinburgh.

Scottish Law Commission (1984). *Breach of confidence*. Report no 90. Cmnd 9385. London: HMSO.
Stair, James Dalrymple, 1st Viscount (1981). *Institutions of the law of Scotland*. 6th ed. Edinburgh: Edinburgh University Press.
Stigler, G., (1971). The theory of economic regulation. *Bell Journal of Economics*, **2**, 3-21.
Tindale, C., (1992). Public attitudes and the treatment of neomorts. In E. Mathews and M. Menlowe (eds), *Philosophy and health care*. Aldershot & Brookfield: Avebury USA:
Tootal, C., (1990). *The law of industrial design*. London: CCH Editions.
Viner, J., (1927). Adam Smith and *laissez faire*. *Journal of Political Economy*, **35**, 198-232.
Von Arnim, E., (1992). *The enchanted April*. London: Virago Press.
Wacks, R., (1989). *Personal information: privacy and the law*. Oxford: Clarendon Press.
Walker, D. M., (1981). *The law of delict in Scotland*. 2nd ed. Edinburgh: W Green.
Whitty, N. R., (1988). Nuisance. In *The laws of Scotland: Stair memorial encyclopedia*, **14**, paras 2001-2168. London and Edinburgh: Butterworths.
Young, E., and Rowan-Robinson, J., (1985). *Scottish planning law and procedure*. Glasgow: Hodge & Co.
Younger Report (1972). *Report of the committee on privacy*. Cmnd 5012. London: HMSO.

ABBREVIATIONS

AllER	*All England Law Reports*
AC	*Appeal Cases* (Decisions of the House of Lords)
Ch	*Chancery Division Law Reports*
D	*Dunlop's Court of Session Reports*
ECR	*European Court Reports*
FSR	*Fleet Street Reports*
F	*Fraser's Court of Session Reports*
IIC	*International Review of Industrial Property and Copyright*
L Ed	*United States Supreme Court Reports Lawyers' Edition*
Mor	*Morison's Dictionary of Decisions of the Court of Session*
NZLR	*New Zealand Law Reports*
OJ EPO	*Official Journal of the European Patent Office*
QB	*Queens Bench Law Reports*
R	*Rettie's Court of Session Reports*
SLR	*Scottish Law Review*
SLT	*Scots Law Times*
SC	*Session Cases*
S Ct	*United States Supreme Court Reports*
US	*United States Supreme Court Reports*
WLR	*Weekly Law Reports*

Note: Law reports are usually published in annual volumes (often more than one per year), and are cited by the relevant year, volume number where appropriate, the abbreviated form of the report series as above, and page number.

HUME
PAPERS ON
PUBLIC POLICY

Published by
Edinburgh University Press

HUME PAPERS ON PUBLIC POLICY

Hume Papers on Public Policy is a new quarterly journal which replaces the series of short monographs previously published by the David Hume Institute under the general title of *Hume Papers*. The journal will be a forum for the publication of first-class research on issues of public policy with especial reference to legal and economic aspects. Some issues will be thematically linked.

Available by subscription or individually through bookshops, it deals with topical issues in a scholarly and accessible way.

Recent Issues have been devoted to:

Sex Equality: Law and Economics:
Examining the development and effect of modern policy and law regarding sex equality, and assessing the future prospects and desirable directions in both policy and law.

Money Laundering:
Examining the topical and exciting subject of money laundering. Five leading commentators and academics tackle the intracacies of international and European Community aspects of money laundering.

1994/95 issues will include:

Scotland and the Union
(Autumn 94)

A team of economists, lawyers, industrialists, historians, journalists and diplomats set out the case for the continuation of the Anglo-Scottish Union of 1707, in whatever form of governmental structure may emerge as the UK moves into the twenty-first century. This book is a forceful argument that Scotland's problems can only be solved in the wider British, European and general international contexts.

Law on the Electronic Frontier
(Winter 1994/95)

An indepth examination of the legal implications of the information technology revolution. Massive data banks threaten individual and society's rights, while computer viruses and the problems of software piracy increasingly cause legal dilemmas. What are the legal consequences of failure in computer-driven safety-critical applications?

In this topical issue, Ian Lloyd and Moira Simpson examine the efficacy of present and proposed legal responses and consider the social, technical and cultural factors influencing computer-related behaviour.

Subscription Rates

Volume 3, 1995
ISSN
1350-7516

Four issues:
January, March,
July, November.

Institutions:

UK and EEC	£68
Overseas	£76
N. America	$116

Individuals:

UK and EEC	£34
Overseas	£38
N. America	$58

Back Issues/
Special Issues
£9.95/ $18

Postage:
Surface postage is included in the subscription. Please add £10 or $18.00 for airmail delivery.

Order Form

Return this form to:

Subscriptions
Edinburgh University Press Ltd
22 George Square
EDINBURGH
EH8 9LF
UK

☐ Please enter my subscription to **Hume Papers on Public Policy, Volume 3, 1995**

☐ I enclose the correct remittance *(please make cheques payable to Edinburgh University Press Ltd.)*

☐ Please debit my Visa/MasterCard account number

_____

Expiry date ___/___

Name ....

Address ....

....

....

Post Code ....

Country ....

Signature:

Date:

Ordering Information

Subscriptions can be accepted for complete volumes only. Prices include packing and surface postage - please add a further £10 / $18 for airmail delivery.

All orders must be accompanied by the correct payment. You can pay by cheque, credit transfer, Unesco coupons, or Visa/MasterCard. Please make your cheques payable to Edinburgh University Press Ltd. Sterling cheques must be drawn on a UK bank account.

The individual rate applies only when a subscription is paid for with a personal cheque or credit card. Back issues are available.

Orders for subscriptions and back issues can be placed by telephone or fax, using your Visa or MasterCard credit cards.

Tel: +44 (0) 131 650 6207
Fax and 24 hrs answerphone:
+44 (0) 131 662 0553

Please ask your library to subscribe to Hume Papers on Public Policy

To: Periodicals Librarian

I recommend a library subscription to Hume Papers on Public Policy

Signature:
Title:
Department: